Ulysses S. Grant: Essays and Documents

Edited by
David L. Wilson
John Y. Simon

Southern Illinois University Press
Carbondale and Edwardsville

LIBRARY OF CONGRESS CATALOGING IN PUBLICATION DATA
Main entry under title:

Ulysses S. Grant: essays and documents.

(Occasional publications/Ulysses S. Grant Association)
Includes index.
Contents: President Grant and the continuing
Civil War/Richard N. Current—Ulysses S. Grant
for today/E. B. Long—"We sail directly for the
Isthmus"/Charles G. Ellington—[etc.]
    1. Grant, Ulysses S. (Ulysses Simpson), 1822–
1885—Addresses, essays, lectures. 2. Presidents—
United States—Biography—Addresses, essays, lectures.
I. Wilson, David L., 1943–   . II. Simon, John Y.
III. Series: Occasional publications (Ulysses S.
Grant Association)
E672.U39   973.8'2   81–18246
ISBN 0-8093-1019-8   AACR2

Contents

Maps and Illustrations

Note on Contributors

RICHARD N. CURRENT, University Distinguished Professor of History at the University of North Carolina at Greensboro, first presented his article as a paper in 1973 at a conference on Ulysses S. Grant sponsored by Northern Illinois University and the Illinois State Historical Society.

CHARLES G. ELLINGTON of Claremont, Calif., for many years a businessman, is now West Coast Regional Director, Office of Economic Adjustment, Office of the Secretary of Defense. His article is adapted from a book he is writing on Grant's experiences on the West Coast.

JOHN M. HOFFMANN, assistant editor of volumes 8 and 9 of *The Papers of Ulysses S. Grant*, is currently librarian of the Illinois Historical Survey at the University of Illinois.

E. B. LONG, one of the nation's most prolific writers on the Civil War, is professor of American studies at the University of Wyoming.

JOHN Y. SIMON, executive director of the Ulysses S. Grant Association since its founding in 1962 and editor of *The Papers of Ulysses S. Grant*, is also professor of history at Southern Illinois University at Carbondale.

DAVID L. WILSON is assistant editor of *The Papers of Ulysses S. Grant* and adjunct assistant professor of history at Southern Illinois University at Carbondale.

HORATIO E. WIRTZ served with the U.S. Army Air Force in Europe during World War II and recently retired from teaching English to high school seniors. Living in New York City, he is currently at work on another article about Grant.

Introduction

In 1973, the Ulysses S. Grant Association *Newsletter* ceased publication. Issued quarterly for a decade, the *Newsletter* had fulfilled its purpose of publicizing the Grant Association in advance of publication of early volumes of *The Papers of Ulysses S. Grant*, the first of which appeared in 1967. The *Newsletter*, however, has been sorely missed as a source of information about the ongoing work of the Grant Association for our members as well as for a more general audience.

Since the demise of the *Newsletter*, volumes 5-8 of the Grant *Papers* have been published by Southern Illinois University Press, and volumes 9-10 have been completed with a projected publication date of fall, 1981. Volumes 11-12 are in preparation and should be delivered to the Press in December, 1981. With the publication of volumes 13-14, the *Papers* will have carried Grant's story past the end of the Civil War. At that point, now in the foreseeable future, we plan to prepare a complete and annotated edition of the *Personal Memoirs of U. S. Grant*, including additional unpublished material in the original manuscript. With this publication schedule and only a small staff, it is easy to understand why the *Newsletter* expired.

During the past few years, the Grant research collection has received a number of major additions through the continuing generosity and support of the Grant family. Mrs. Edith Grant Griffiths, Mrs. John S. Dietz, and Mrs. Paul E. Ruestow recently donated a large number of books, scrapbooks, and miscellaneous material which had been part of the collection of their father, Ulysses S. Grant 3rd. Chapman Grant, son of Jesse R. Grant and grandson of the president, has provided the association with some family correspondence and a large collection of scrapbooks on the Grant family, containing numerous clippings, photographs, and letters. In addition, Special Collections of Morris Library at Southern Illinois University recently acquired parts of the original drafts of Grant's sixth and eighth annual messages to Congress. The eighth annual message is particularly noteworthy because of Grant's statement concerning mistakes made during his two terms as president. Mrs. Ann Wenzlick—a long-time resident of White Haven, the home of Julia Dent Grant in St. Louis—gave the association a number of books, photographs, and articles concerning Grant, as well as documents and correspondence concerning White Haven.

The *Newsletter* fulfilled another important function by making possible the publication of numerous brief essays and documents bearing on Grant's life which were inappropriate or impossible to include within the Grant *Papers*. This book contains articles and documents covering a wide range of topics, all contributions toward the study of Grant. Such an outlet is important for Grant scholarship, and we plan to continue the series to meet this need.

This book has an additional purpose. In recent years, revolutionary changes have occurred in publishing. The electronic era is upon us, and we need to learn something about computer-assisted text-processing and printing methods. Consequently, this book is an experiment for the editors using text-processing equipment to generate a computer-prepared tape from which the printer can produce camera-ready copy. The editors, it must be admitted, have been somewhat skeptical of a publication system that has as one of its major links a telephone line. Electronic pulses mystify us. But learn we must.

Of course, this book could not have emerged without the assistance of people who do understand the functioning of electronic systems—gremlins and all. We are particularly indebted to Allan Jones, assistant coordinator of University Graphics at Southern Illinois University, who provided the knowledge and guidance (plus enthusiasm) necessary for our encounter with the mysteries of the computer. We are also indebted to Richard W. Neal, production director of Southern Illinois University Press, without whose support and interest (not to mention his book design), nothing could have been accomplished. Frank G. Burke, executive director of the National Historical Publications and Records Commission, sponsor of *The Papers of Ulysses S. Grant*, has encouraged experiments with modern technology. We thank Sue E. Dotson, editorial assistant for the Grant Association, for part of the typing and numerous editorial suggestions, along with Kathy Rodgers, a student worker who spent many hours before a Decwriter. We also thank Patrick M. McCoy, Tamara Melia, and Eric A. Topham, graduate assistants for the Grant Association, for proofreading.

DAVID L. WILSON
JOHN Y. SIMON

I

President Grant and the Continuing Civil War

By Richard N. Current

"Let us have peace." That was the plea of Ulysses S. Grant, a plea he made at the beginning of his presidency and repeated from time to time thereafter. "Let us have peace." But President Grant stuck to his "Southern policy," and as a consequence there was no peace so long as he remained in office. He ended his second term with a sense of frustration and defeat. In his eighth and last annual message to Congress he did something that few if any other outgoing presidents have ever done: he confessed that he had made "mistakes."

This touch of candor—so utterly lacking in our chief magistrates of more recent times—ought perhaps to have disarmed historians and given them a little charity in judging President Grant. It has, of course, done nothing of the sort. Instead, it has been taken as a self-confirmation of wrongheadedness and incompetence. When the late Arthur M. Schlesinger polled his fellow historians, in 1948 and again in 1962, they rated Grant on both occasions as one of two "failures" among all the presidents, placing him next to the very bottom of the list, only a notch above Warren G. Harding.

Those whom the historians ranked the highest were the *war* presidents, with Abraham Lincoln at the top. On this ground alone, if on no other, Grant deserves reconsideration, for he too may be viewed as a war president. He was commander in chief during the Reconstruction phase of the continuing Civil War.

A possible renewal of hostilities had been far from General Grant's thoughts when, at Appomattox, he gave his generous terms to the surrendering army of Robert E. Lee. "I am satisfied that the mass of thinking men of the South accept the present situation of affairs in good faith," Grant wrote a little later, after his southern tour in the summer of 1865. "The questions which have heretofore divided the sentiments of the people of the two sections—slavery and States' rights, or the right of a State to secede from the Union—they regard as having been settled forever by the highest tribunal—arms—that man can resort to." But Grant's friend William T. Sherman took a quite different view, predicting a kind of guerrilla war. "Now," Sherman said, after his even more liberal terms to Joseph E. Johnston had been overruled, ". . . we will have to deal with numberless bands of desperadoes, headed by such men as Mosby, Forrest . . . and others, who know not and care not for danger and its consequences." Time was to prove Sherman's prediction accurate.

General Grant began to change his mind as President Andrew Johnson defied Congress and persisted in trying to restore the Southern states according to his own plan. This involved the return of ex-Confederates to office, the passage of the black codes to provide a substitute for slavery, vetoes of congressional bills for assuring civil rights and protection to the freedmen, riots in which blacks and loyal whites were the victims, and the rise of the Ku Klux Klan. In the fall of 1866, as the congressional elections approached, it seemed to Grant that Johnson had aroused the lately subdued rebels to a point where a military clash with the adherents of Congress was a real possibility. "Commanders in Southern States," he advised Major General Philip H. Sheridan, "will have to take great care to see, if a crisis does come, that no armed headway can be made against the Union."

By the time the first Reconstruction Act was passed, in March of 1867, Grant was ready to give his full endorsement to its provisions, Negro suffrage and all. His conversion to the suffrage cause had resulted neither from a love for Southern blacks nor from a hatred of Southern whites. He now had no more vindictiveness toward his late enemies than he had had at Appomattox. His conversion to black enfranchisement was like his earlier conversion to black emancipation. In 1862 he had faced the question of what to do with the thousands of slave refugees flocking into his Tennessee camp. Though no abolitionist in principle, he then decided that he must not return the slaves to their owners but must set them free so as to weaken the enemy and win the war. Similarly, in 1867, he concluded that giving the suffrage to the freedmen was (to quote Adam Badeau) "the only practical means of securing what had been won in the field." Otherwise, the late rebels of the South in combination with the "Copperheads" of the North would regain control of the federal government, and "the results of the war would be lost."

After his inauguration, President Grant reversed the obstructionist tactics of President Johnson and set out to execute wholeheartedly the congressional Reconstruction plan. He was enthusiastic when the plan was capped by the Fifteenth Amendment, so enthusiastic that he departed from custom to announce the ratification in a special message, on March 30, 1870. In a sentence breathtaking both for its length and for its exaggeration, he declared:

"A measure which makes at once 4,000,000 people voters who were heretofore declared by the highest tribunal in the land not citizens of the United States, nor eligible to become so (with the assertion that 'at the time of the Declaration of Independence the opinion was fixed and universal in the civilized portion of the white race, regarded as an axiom in morals as well as in politics, that black men had no rights which the white man was bound to respect' [a quotation, of course, from Chief Justice Roger B. Taney's opinion in the Dred Scott case, of 1857]), is indeed a measure of grander importance than any other one act of the kind from the foundation of our free Government to the present day."

Very few Southern whites shared Grant's enthusiasm for the Fifteenth Amendment. This amendment, together with the reconstruction acts, only intensified the spirit of rebellion in the South. The campaign of violence and terror increased, with the aim of depriving the freedmen of the vote, overthrowing the reconstructed state governments, and thus frustrating federal law. The masked night-riders of the Klan and other Klan-like groups had their day and then were succeeded by less ritualistic but even more effective organizations of armed and mounted men, such as the White Leagues of Louisiana, the rifle clubs of Mississippi, and the Red Shirts of South Carolina.

By 1870–71, Grant confronted a situation resembling the one that Lincoln had faced a decade earlier, and Grant responded to it in much the same way. Like Lincoln, he invoked an old statute of 1795 which authorized the president, "in case of an insurrection in any state," to "call out the militia of any state to suppress such insurrection." He soon felt, however, that he needed powers more specifically designed for dealing with the existing disorders in the South. Accordingly, Congress passed a series of three "force acts," which empowered him to use military and other means to enforce the Fourteenth and Fifteenth Amendments wherever "unlawful combinations and conspiracies" were to be found, and which declared such combinations and conspiracies to be "rebellion against the Government of the United States." In successive proclamations invoking these acts from 1870 to 1876, Grant used language reminiscent of Lincoln's in 1861. Again, a president was calling upon troops to put down "combinations" that could not be "controlled or suppressed by the ordinary course of justice."

Until the end of Grant's second term the federal troops remaining at Southern posts were kept fairly busy in assisting civilian officials, especially at election times. More than two hundred detachments were made in a single year. In nine counties of South Carolina the president, under the authority of the force acts, briefly suspended the writ of habeas corpus and imposed martial law. He used the army to the greatest extent in Louisiana, where, as he said, the "lawlessness, turbulence, and bloodshed" were the worst. When the Louisiana Democrats threatened to make good their claim to victory in the 1872 election, he dispatched soldiers to New Orleans to protect William Pitt Kellogg's Republican regime. He sent them again after the Democrats and their White League allies had killed dozens of black and white Republicans in the Colfax and Coushatta massacres, had risen in armed revolt, and had driven Kellogg and his followers out of the statehouse.

Southern conservative newspapers kept denouncing Grant and complaining of federal "tyranny and despotism." Northern Democratic papers called him "Kaiser Ulysses" and said he was "puffed up with a sense of his despotic authority." Anti-Grant Republicans talked about his assumption of "enormous and irresponsible powers" and warned against the dangers of "Caesarism"—or "Grantism," which to his critics meant much the same thing. The Democratic and Liberal Republican propaganda gave the impression that the president, out of sheer cussedness, was making war on the people of the South. No doubt this propaganda helped to account for Northern disillusionment with the whole idea of Reconstruction. It helped to account also for the Democrats' gains in the elections of 1874, gains which gave them control of the national House of Representatives in 1875.

Nothing could have been farther off the mark than the charges of militaristic excess against Grant. The truth is that, in the execution of his Southern policy, he showed remarkable self-restraint. Only in a small area and only for a short period did he resort to martial law. On several occasions, despite urgent appeals, he held back military aid and tried to settle electoral disputes by mediation. On other occasions he sent troops not to assist Republicans against Democrats but merely to keep the two from going into armed combat with one another. He was quick, perhaps at times too quick, to withdraw the soldiers once the immediate threat to law and order had appeared to subside.

Thus, in the case of Louisiana, he might have prevented the worst of the violence if, from the beginning of the trouble in that state, he had maintained a large force there and had ordered it to break up the pretended government and the paramilitary organizations of the Democrats. From New Orleans, Sheridan begged for permission to treat the White Leaguers as "banditti"—to shoot them as outlaws. There was (at least as seen in retrospect) a good deal of merit in Sheridan's proposal, but the president declined even to consider it, though appreciating the general's point of view.

Grant kept his use of military force to a minimum for several reasons. For one thing, he had constitutional and legal scruples—which were reinforced when the strict constructionist Edwards Pierrepont became his attorney general in 1875—and he was willing to take action only when assured that it was within the letter of the law. Then, too, he had doubts about the rights and wrongs in some of the electoral disputes, where fraud appeared to be rife on both sides, and these doubts gave him pause. Moreover, he had to take into account the swell of adverse opinion in the North. Thus, in 1875, when the desperate Republicans of Mississippi were pleading in vain for federal support,

Attorney General Pierrepont sent them a telegram that quoted Grant as saying: "The whole public are tired out with these annual autumnal outbreaks in the South, and the great majority are ready now to condemn any interference on the part of the Government." Besides, after the congressional elections of 1874, Grant was handicapped by the predominance of Democrats in the House. They tried to embarrass him with calls for information about his use of soldiers, and they turned down his request for new legislation—for yet another force act—which would have clarified and amplified his power to employ the army.

Finally, even if Grant had been inclined to intervene more actively than he was, he would have been limited by the unavailability of troops. The total of those stationed in the South had shrunk from nearly 200,000 in mid-1865 to about 11,000 in late 1869 and only 6,000 at the end of 1876. These 6,000 were widely scattered in small garrisons. After the disputed 1876 election, Grant declared that "if there had been more military force available" he would have been justified in using it in several of the Southern states.

Restrained though he was in resorting to military might, Grant held deep convictions about what he considered the basic issues of the conflict in the South. One was the issue of actual freedom for the former slaves. The question whether the Fourteenth and Fifteenth Amendments were to be "practically enforced," a convention of Alabama blacks declared in 1874, was a question whether emancipation was to be a "reality or a mockery" and whether the blacks themselves were to be "freemen in fact or only in name." At almost exactly the same time, Grant was saying, in response to complaints about "interference by Federal authority," that if the Fifteenth Amendment and the force acts did not provide for such interference, then they were "without meaning" and the "whole scheme of colored enfranchisement" was "worse than mockery and little better than a crime."

At stake was not only freedom but also Union, as Grant saw the matter. It was a question "whether the control of the Government should be thrown immediately into the hands of those who had so recently and persistently tried to destroy it," he said in his last annual message to Congress. "Reconstruction, as finally agreed upon, means this and only this, except that the late slave was enfranchised, giving an increase, as was supposed, to the Union-loving and Union-supporting votes. If *free* in the full sense of the word [and Grant underlined the word *free*], they would not disappoint this expectation."

By 1877, the Republicans of Mississippi had already fallen before the terrorism of the Democrats. In the three Southern states where Republicans still managed to hold on, they did so only with the support of federal troops. Grant kept these soldiers in place to the very end of his presidency. Then he saw, with dismay and disgust, his Southern policy reversed by his successor, Rutherford B. Hayes. Under Hayes, the troops were removed, the force acts ignored, and the Fourteenth and Fifteenth Amendments nullified. For the rest of the century the Republicans talked off and on of enforcement but did nothing about it. By the early 1900s, all but seven of the forty-two sections of the three force acts had been repealed or superseded or declared unconstitutional, and the seven remaining sections were dead letters.

Writing in the early 1900s, historian William A. Dunning said: "Grant in 1868 had cried peace, but in his time, with the radicals and carpet-baggers in the saddle, there was no peace; with Hayes peace came." Dunning and his followers (along with nearly all their white contemporaries, Northern as well as Southern, Republican as well as Democratic) were convinced that the attempt to impose Negro suffrage on the South had been a horrible mistake. According to those historians, the attempt had provoked such disorder and violence as actually existed in the South. But the lawlessness, they said, was exaggerated for "political effect," to suit the propaganda needs of the Radical Republicans. Insofar as the Ku Klux Klan and similar organizations had a "political motive" of their own, Dunning insisted, this "was concerned with purely local incidents of radical misrule, and was ridiculously remote from any purpose that could be fairly called 'rebellion' against the United States."

Though "peace" (in the Dunning view) did not come until 1877, the war itself had long since ended. The Civil War was one thing and the Reconstruction quite another—an unfortunate aftermath, a sequel and yet a kind of non sequitur. For all its undeniable aspects of meanness, the Civil War was a credit to both sides, and the participants were ennobled by courage, sacrifice, and high ideals. But Reconstruction disgraced the victors. Not content with winning the war, preserving the Union, and emancipating the slaves, a ruling faction of Northern vindictives proceeded to "reconstruct" and, in the process, to humiliate and despoil the already ruined and chastened South. These Republican Radicals, thousands of them, now invaded the defeated land. They went as penniless adventurers, as "carpetbaggers," to mislead the newly enfranchised Negro, misgovern the reconstructed states, and misappropriate whatever wealth remained. Thus, in the role of conqueror, the greedy politician replaced the brave soldier: the jackal came in the track of the lion. More than the war itself, this time of terrible peace embittered the Southern people and left lasting scars upon their memory.

Such, in outline, is the story as Dunning, James Ford Rhodes, and most other writers once told it. That version still has its believers, and no doubt it contains some elements of historical truth, but we may question whether it represents the whole truth, or even the essential truth. There is another way of looking at the events of the 1860s and the 1870s. This way, we may discover at least a few significant themes that extend from the wartime through the "postwar" period and give a common character to both. Thus we may see Reconstruction as essentially a continuation of the Civil War.

One continuing theme is violence. The war was not to be ended by a treaty, of course, or even by a general cease-fire agreement (though that was the kind of agreement that Sherman hoped to make with Johnston). Repeatedly President Lincoln had said the war would cease, on the part of his government, when it had ceased on the part of those who were resisting the government's authority. The rebels had only to lay down their arms. Though the Confederate armies surrendered in 1865, the South remained an "occupied country," and before long it showed signs of being a hostile one as well. President Johnson proposed to withdraw the occupying troops, and on August 20, 1866, he proclaimed that peace had been restored in all the states formerly in rebellion. This proclamation the Supreme Court later took as marking the legal end of hostilities.

Yet, throughout the South, resistance to federal authority continued on the part of well-armed and well-organized bodies of men. With uniformed, gun-wielding horsemen on the prowl, it was sometimes hard to tell the difference between a political and a military campaign. So, if formal fighting ended in 1865 and legal hostilities in 1866, irregular warfare went on for years afterward. And if, during these years, there was no such wholesale bloodshed as at Antietam or Gettysburg, there were nevertheless a great many casualties in countless engagements of one kind and another.

A second continuing theme is personnel. Confederate veterans made up the core of the persisting opposition to federal authority in the South. Nathan Bedford Forrest, the one-time slavetrader who had gained fame as a commander of Confederate cavalry, founded and led the Ku Klux Klan. The berobed Klansmen pretended to be ghosts of the Confederate dead but were, in considerable numbers, flesh-and-blood survivors of the Confederate army. Former rebel soldiers also officered and manned the rifle companies such as the Red Shirts, whose hero and guiding spirit, Wade Hampton, had been like Forrest a leader of Southern cavalry.

On the other side, the army of occupation consisted largely of men who had served in earlier compaigns against the Confederates. Small and scattered as this force was, its members often were remote from the scenes of actual combat. More active than the regular soldiers, on the new firing lines, were the carpetbaggers and their scalawag and Negro allies, sometimes organized as state militia. The carpetbaggers were, almost to a man, veterans of the Union army. Whatever else they may have been, they were men who formerly had worn the blue, and they now had to pit themselves against men who, whether at present wearing white robes or red shirts, once had worn the gray.

A third continuing theme is purpose. By 1865, the North had not yet quite achieved its war aims of Union and freedom. Not that the rebel Southerners intended to try secession again, but they did intend to go on running their own affairs, with as little interference as possible from the outside. The war from 1861 to 1865, though bringing about the collapse of the Confederacy, had not destroyed but strengthened the belief in state rights and the sense of sectional distinctiveness, and the sense of devotion to the South. Though no longer fighting for their national independence, the Southerners, in resisting Reconstruction, were fighting for their separate identity and for a large measure of local and regional autonomy.

Nor did the Southerners propose to reestablish the institution of chattel slavery, though they had gone to war in 1861 to preserve it. At that time the vice president of the Confederacy, Alexander H. Stephens, was only stating the obvious when he declared that the idea of Negro inferiority, with its institutional expression, Negro slavery, formed the "corner-stone" of the new government. This cornerstone remained after the rest of the edifice had collapsed: the dogma of racial inequality survived the defeat of the Confederacy. The black codes, together with other outrages against the Negro, convinced the Radical Republicans that the freedman would have to be given civil and political rights if he was to be truly free. The conservative Southerners were determined to cancel those rights and, as they put it, to restore "white supremacy." With them, it was a matter of maintaining customs and institutions that would correspond to the belief in black inferiority.

Taking into account the continuity of violence, of personnel, and of aims, we may look upon Lee's surrender as more a transitional than a terminal point. At that time (in April, 1865) the Lost Cause was not yet wholly lost, the Union victory not yet fully won. Afterwards there might have been much less bitterness and bloodshed if President Johnson had got away with his program for a quick and easy peace. But in that case the South would have been, to a considerable extent, victorious in defeat. In the end the South was to be partly victorious despite the passage of the Radical Reconstruction plan. The Compromise of 1877 left the former slaves to their former masters, and the South pretty much to itself.

That was not the fault of Ulysses S. Grant. That was not the outcome that he wanted to see. But the conquering hero of the Civil War failed in his efforts to confirm the victory through Reconstruction.

Grant's low repute among historians has been largely a product of the Dunning school. His fame continues to suffer even though the Dunning interpretation as a whole has long been discredited. It is time that revisionist scholars, having already revised practically every other phase of Reconstruction, should reconsider the role of President Grant.

There can be no doubt that, in the future, he will rank much higher than he has done in the past. If he was not one of the more successful war presidents, he was, in a certain respect, one of the greatest, if not the greatest of all presidents. In this respect, only Lyndon B. Johnson can even be compared with him. None of the others carried on such a determined struggle, against such hopeless odds, to give reality to the Fourteenth and Fifteenth Amendments and to protect all citizens of this country in the exercise of their constitutional rights.

II

Ulysses S. Grant for Today

By E. B. Long

He was the brutal, unfeeling drunkard who accidentally helped win the Civil War by needlessly butchering men. He was a very commonplace, crude, unimaginative sort of dolt who had a lot of good luck. Then, of course, Ulysses S. Grant is way down on the list of real generals when compared to such as R. E. Lee and Stonewall Jackson.

He never made a dime, had failed miserably in the old army. His sins went beyond just drink while he was on the Pacific Coast. After the Civil War he was involved in a shabby role in the struggle between President Andrew Johnson and Secretary of War Edwin M. Stanton. And then he became president only because he was a war hero and the people were tired of politicians. His presidency was an utter disaster.

After his two terms, Grant toured the world as a rather comic conquering hero and returned home to try again, selfishly, for the Republican nomination and a third term. As a businessman he was a complete bust and was only rescued from the poorhouse by the charity of his friends. He did not actually write his *Memoirs*. A letter printed in *Harper's Weekly* once described him as "The drunken Democrat whom the Republicans dragged out of the Galena gutter, besmeared with the blood of his countrymen slain in domestic broil, and lifted to a high pedestal as Moloch of their worship, rules . . . over the prostrate ruins of WASHINGTON's republic."[1] He was, in short, a nasty, whiskey-drinking old man. Many of these canards are still with us in one form or another.

On the other hand, you know that Grant was a paragon of virtue suffering from the criticism of small minds, jealousy, and the failings of inaccurate

---

1. *Harper's Weekly*, XXI (Jan. 6, 1877), 12.

historians. He was not a drunkard. In fact, he may never have taken a drink. He had left the army and the West Coast because he was homesick, being the personification of a homebody. He had some ill luck just before the war. He was in fact a partner in his family's Galena leather store. When war came he had to fight for a chance and showed tremendous growth, but the talent was there all the time. He was a master of strategy, tactics, and in handling men. He was far superior to Lee; he beat him, didn't he? Far from being a butcher, he was acutely sensitive to losses. He won the Vicksburg campaign, opening the Mississippi, and he did it primarily by cutting loose from his base. In Virginia he ignored Lincoln and went his own way, with pertinacity and super-vision. In victory he was magnanimous. He restored the postwar army to an effective force for the new role it was to play. As president, while there were scandals, not a cent ever came to Grant. He has been greatly maligned.

He was received as the personification of the ideal American on his triumphal world tour. He bowed to the urging of supporters in trying for a third term. He wrote the entire *Memoirs* despite a fatal illness. His was the archetypical American success story of a man who appears common on the surface but who runs very, very deep. One could go on and on.

Now, we may well consider Ulysses S. Grant for today, to attempt to sort out the true attributes from the fictitious. It is well over a century ago this April that the peach trees blossoming on the Tennessee River were blasted by the guns of Shiloh. It is over a century ago that he won two terms for the presidency. This man was president of the United States for eight years and he must be considered a vital factor in the North's winning the Civil War. His career can perhaps show us a good deal about ourselves as Americans.

While it is important for historians to investigate a man's early life, there is a temptation to read too much into the formative years. Lincoln has suffered from this. His log cabin youth was certainly not unusual for his day.

Grant was not raised in a log cabin, but in modest, though decent, surroundings. His Ohio boyhood seems very normal. He detested school, and was fond of horses and animals, not unusual traits for small boys. He disliked working in his father's tannery, but how many sons have aversions to the family business? He didn't like his formal name—Hiram Ulysses Grant, but then I am not too fond of mine.

He was unhappy about going to West Point, and earnestly hoped the place would burn down. While there he accepted the name mixup which left him permanently Ulysses S. Grant. He liked some of his studies, disliked others. He indulged in a normal number of pranks, displayed no embryo genius, nor was he a hopeless failure as a cadet. He graduated in 1843, twenty-first in a class of thirty-nine. In the Mexican War Grant gave his efforts to the tasks assigned him and occasionally, as at Monterrey and the gates of Mexico City, he showed considerable imagination and perception. He fell in love with Julia Dent and henceforth enjoyed her family probably more than his own.

Then came the years as a soldier on the West Coast. What about them? The tale about his having fathered an Indian child can probably be dismissed.[2] It is obvious from his letters to his wife that he was homesick. These letters display a pedestrian, warm expression of family love.[3]

In 1854 he resigned from the army. So did a good many others for one reason or another. Grant probably was not mistreated by stupid superiors, but was simply tired of stagnation and was painfully homesick. Also, I am convinced he was doing some drinking at this time, not an unusual custom among soldiers.

Let us face this question of Grant and liquor before we go further. It is peculiar how defensive Grant scholars become on this subject (even though they may imbibe modestly themselves). Grant did drink. Let's accept that. There is enough documentary evidence to show it. But does that mean he was an alcoholic? Of course not. If he had been a sot, there is very little likelihood we would ever have heard of him. Drunks, such as he has been labeled, do not rise to the heights of military leadership or to the presidency.

One undocumentable speculation is that Grant probably could not hold his liquor. Another, more important, is that on not one single occasion have I found documentation that drink ever interfered with his duties or was a factor when important decisions were required or the going was rough. I am convinced reporter Sylvanus Cadwallader is at least partly correct that Grant was drunk at Satartia in 1863 during the Vicksburg campaign.[4] He may or may not have been under the influence when he accidently lost his false teeth off the headquarters boat and had to write home for new ones. I am convinced he was somewhat intoxicated after Vicksburg when he fell from a fractious horse in New Orleans in early September, 1863, and was painfully injured.[5] There may have been a few other instances, but we have to weigh the influence of these falls from grace. Study shows they came at somewhat relaxed times during the war, when Grant's temporary incapacity didn't matter. His presidency shows no sign of a lush in the White House.

Of course, these incidents of drinking couldn't be hidden. How preposterous it is to say, as it has been said, that General Benjamin F. Butler was kept in command as long as he was, despite his uncanny ineptitude in things

2. Thomas M. Anderson to Hamlin Garland, Nov. 25, 1897, Hamlin Garland Papers, University of Southern California, Los Angeles, Calif.
3. John Y. Simon, ed., *The Papers of Ulysses S. Grant* (Carbondale and Edwardsville, Ill., 1967–), I, *passim* (hereafter cited as *PUSG*).
4. Benjamin P. Thomas, ed., *Three Years with Grant as Recalled by War Correspondent Sylvanus Cadwallader* (New York, 1955), 102–12.
5. Maj. Gen. Nathaniel P. Banks to Mrs. Banks, Sept. 6, 1863, Nathaniel P. Banks Papers, Library of Congress; Maj. Gen. William B. Franklin to Brig. Gen. William F. Smith, Dec. 28, 1863, Papers of William F. Smith, private collection of Walter Wilgus. For details see analysis in Bruce Catton, *Grant Takes Command* (Boston and Toronto, 1969), 22–25; E. B. Long, "Research Notes for Bruce Catton's *Centennial History of the Civil War*," Library of Congress.

military, because he held Grant's weakness over the general in chief's head. Everyone in the North and probably in the South had heard the stories. It is nonsense to think Lincoln would have trusted Grant so far if he had felt alcohol controlled him. Enough of this. The question must not be avoided but put in some perspective.

True, when Ulysses left the army under a cloud, he floundered a bit for nearly six years. Other old army men who later made their mark were the same in many respects. When Jesse Grant had his son go up to Galena, Illinois, in May of 1860, it was not to some sort of exile, though it is often considered so. Jesse was a hard businessman, the family leather store was active. Why not keep it in the family? Besides, one of Grant's brothers was suffering severely from terminal tuberculosis. It was a natural move. Grant was not a mere errand boy or clerk. He was as much a partner as Jesse would allow. He got out on his own and collected debts. His bent for meticulous detail he used to advantage. If the war had not come along, he might eventually have run the business.

Thus, the early years look, upon close examination, to be pretty average. There is nothing unusual, either, about Grant's getting back into the army. He had only minimum political pull, was not known as a party partisan, and was not aggressive. But he was an old army man and when the war started even his modest experience took on increased value. Everyone, even mediocrities, was of use.

He did show, as he should have, a skill at discipline when he quickly subdued his unruly, untrained 21st Illinois regiment and created a military unit out of a bunch of country roughs. He revealed a trait that was common with him—succinctness. And he showed the men he meant to tolerate no nonsense. He also displayed ability in marching those unsoldierly soldiers from Illinois to Missouri. Yet that wasn't any more than could be expected from an old army captain.

His career in Missouri in the summer of 1861 was that of a fairly competent commander of small forces of occupation. He didn't get into any trouble, and there wasn't much opportunity for exhibiting any brilliance. Grant was named a brigadier, but countless other officers of the prewar army, most now forgotten, came back in at such ranks.

John Charles Frémont, in Union command in the West, was wary of Southern operations in southeastern Missouri. Frémont, of the extravagant headquarters, of the colorful Hungarian-speaking bodyguard, had never-modest dreams of grandeur for himself and his frightening wife Jessie Benton Frémont. Frémont needed someone at Cairo, Illinois, to help settle the place down and to advance his melodramatic, unrealistic scheme of moving rapidly down the Mississippi and, nearly single-handed, winning the war in the West by late fall.[6]

Grant was unhappy about shifting his headquarters again, which prevented him from having his family with him. But, on September 4, 1861, he unobtrusively took over in Cairo. This period of Grant's career is usually just mentioned by most authors, who then rapidly move on to the engagement at Belmont, Missouri, on the Mississippi, November 7, 1861, which is probably described correctly as the first real battle training ground for Grant. I used to see it this way.

But I would like to submit that Grant's first, and one of his most important independent actions was his seizure of Paducah, Kentucky, two months earlier, on September 6.[7]

Unrealistically established at the start of the war, the neutrality of Kentucky was both an irritant and a benefit to North and South. Lincoln handled the situation dexterously. The North was violating that neutrality possibly even more than the Confederacy, despite denials.

On the third and fourth of September, 1861, Bishop and General Leonidas Polk ordered Gideon Pillow's Confederates to move out of Tennessee, up the Mississippi to occupy Hickman and Columbus, Kentucky. Columbus was vital.[8] Its high bluffs, some twenty miles south of the Federal base at Cairo, commanded the river. For long years Polk has been blamed for a significant violation of Kentucky neutrality. But, actually, Polk believed Frémont was planning a similar move, and the Confederate general was correct. Frémont gave Grant indications that he intended to attack Columbus and, without orders from Washington, invade Kentucky on his own.[9] Federal troops were already in Missouri across from Columbus.

On September 5 a scout or spy of Frémont's, Charles de Arnaud, managed to get to Cairo and told of the Confederate invasion.[10] Instead of moving toward conflict with Polk at well-defended Columbus, Grant immediately set in motion to go some forty miles up the Ohio to Paducah at the mouth of the Tennessee River, not far from the mouth of the Cumberland. He telegraphed

---

6. Frémont Memoirs, ms., John C. Frémont Papers, Bancroft Library, University of California, Berkeley, Calif. (hereafter cited as Frémont Memoirs); U.S. War Department, *The War of the Rebellion: A Compilation of the Official Records of the Union and Confederate Armies* (Washington, 1880–1901), I, iii, 141–42 (hereafter cited as *O.R.* followed by series and vol.; *Personal Memoirs of U. S. Grant* (New York, 1885–86), I, 261 (hereafter cited as *Memoirs*).

7. See E. B. Long, "The Paducah Affair," *The Register of the Kentucky Historical Society*, 70, 4 (Oct., 1972), 253–76; Bruce Catton, *Grant Moves South* (Boston and Toronto, 1960), 48–50.

8. *O.R.*, I, iv, 181.

9. *Ibid.*, I, iii, 142; Fremont Memoirs.

10. *Memoirs*, I, 264–65; *PUSG*, II, 193.

Frémont of his intentions and said he would proceed unless ordered otherwise.[11] In a matter of hours, 1,800 troops on transports and the two converted wooden gunboats *Tyler* and *Conestoga* left Cairo, steamed up the Ohio, and landed on the morning of September 6 at Paducah. Grant took the largely hostile but unresisting city. Only one shot was fired and that by accident from a gunboat. Confederate troops were said to have been nearby, but that they were is not certain. Polk had known he should have gone to Paducah overland from Columbus, but was held up in doing so. Now it was too late. The Federals fortified the city and in a day or two took Smithland at the mouth of the Cumberland.[12] On paper it didn't look like much, just a town in Kentucky occupied as a counter to the Confederates.

When Grant returned to Cairo the same day, he found there permission from Frémont to do what he had already done. Thereafter Frémont and Jessie characteristically tried to take credit for the ploy.[13] Grant had quietly, quickly, and on his own taken an enormous strategic step. It was not so much that he had seen the opportunity, but that he had acted upon it.

I submit it is possible, even probable, that the whole future of the war in the West was altered by this, Grant's first major action. If the Confederates had done nothing more than seize and hold the Ohio and Mississippi River line from Columbus to Paducah, the February, 1862, Henry-Donelson campaign on the Tennessee border would not have occurred when it did. Yankee shipping on the Ohio would have been severed. Federals would have had to cross the Ohio by an amphibious assault force or go around the end. If the Confederates could also have occupied other strong points, as they possibly could have done, all along the Ohio, the northern boundary of the Confederacy would have been on the Ohio instead of farther south. The political and social impact of such a Confederate move would have been tremendous. The Confederates would have held a defense line much, much stronger than the attenuated one they did establish, which was well anchored at Columbus and Cumberland Gap, but weak and disconnected in the long miles stretching across southern Kentucky. The Union would have had another state to cross in its invasion of the South. Kentucky would have been firmly within the Confederacy and probably far more native sons would have joined the Southern armies.

But it didn't happen that way. Grant took Paducah, proving that all determining military operations do not need to be stupendous extravaganzas and bloodbaths.

While his staff members, with the exception of John A. Rawlins, were

11. *Ibid.*; *O.R.*, I, iii, 150.
12. *Memoirs*, I, 265–66; *O.R.*, I, iv, 196–97.
13. Frémont Memoirs, 256–57; *PUSG*, II, 191–92.

never renowned for their efficiency, Grant himself showed capability as a desk general. He used commonplace, ordinary horse sense in developing Cairo as the major base it became in the fall and winter of 1861–62.

Grant was learning to be a commanding general. He was being given, by the luck of the draw and turn of events, the time to learn more about the trade. Some Civil War generals never had such a chance. One associate said that "Grant at Cairo was not an assertive man; didn't interfere with small affairs. He was always deprecatory in manner; never asserted his authority. He was always looking for big results; no time to waste on formalities. . . ."[14]

Then, in February, 1862, came the Tennessee and Cumberland River campaign, the fighting for Forts Henry and Donelson. Grant did see the idea of moving up the two rivers into the heartland of the upper South, but so, too, did a host of other people. No one has untangled who deserves the credit, if there is any to deserve. It is strange that so many superficial histories give Grant some credit for Fort Henry, which was taken by the gunboats under Flag Officer Andrew H. Foote on February 6, while Grant's army a few miles away was slogging through the mud.

After the fall of Fort Henry, Grant felt he had to delay his attack on Fort Donelson so the gunboats could get around from the Tennessee to the Cumberland to aid him. By this fortuitous delay, Grant was enabled to capture a good many thousand more Confederates on February 16 than if he had moved in earlier because Confederate Albert Sidney Johnston was foolishly pouring troops into the really indefensible fort. It seems that luck perhaps played a small role in Grant's spectacular victory.

But it was Grant on his own, to some extent violating the letter of command boundaries, who pressed on to Nashville, recognizing the main city of central Tennessee to be a primary goal of the war in the West.[15] The taking of Nashville has not always received the attention it deserves. There is nothing too impressive about the capture of an undefended supply and manpower depot. Grant wasn't the only one who recognized the extreme value of Nashville, but he was one of several who did something about it.

Then came the spring of 1862 and those blossoming peach trees along the Tennessee River near a shabby hamlet called Pittsburg Landing and a meeting house called Shiloh. I don't think any historian can prove that Grant's unprotected, unprepared army was not surprised by Albert Sidney Johnston's Confederates. A Federal defeat on the field was a very near thing. Grant should have been at Pittsburg Landing and not north in the Cherry Mansion at Savannah, Tennessee. He had grown perceptibly as a commander in less than a year's time, but he was not growing at Shiloh. He later ducked

14. Interview with John McElroy, Garland Papers.
15. For summary of the complicated situation, see Catton, *Grant Moves South*, 189–91.

the question of surprise and even wrote, lamely, that "drill and discipline were worth more to our men than fortifications."[16] This was only one of his weak defenses for not entrenching and being more alert. Grant suffered public criticism for Shiloh, some of which he deserved. On the other hand, I can find no evidence that he was drunk before or during the battle. Shiloh was part of his training ground. Grant never made quite these same mistakes again.

After Shiloh we move into a rather uncharacteristic period of depression for Grant. Placed second in command to Henry Wager Halleck, in the march from Shiloh to Corinth, Mississippi, Grant chafed and stewed. Some of the quiet strength seemed gone. He now had to work directly under a superior on the field, something he had not done before in this war and was not to do again. It seems a fair judgment that Grant performed better when on his own. He generally obeyed orders meticulously, but usually his superiors were in St. Louis or Washington. Not that his was an arrogant independence—far from it. It was an independence born of self-consciousness, his need to think things out himself in that straight-line way that was so typical of him.

The summer and fall of 1862 show another period of competent command, in what amounted to control of the area of Federal occupation. By mid-July of 1862, he was in command along the Mississippi when Halleck went east as general in chief.

Grant was not the originator of the Vicksburg campaigns of 1862 and 1863. The idea had been in many minds, and to credit him with the conception is to distort. Throughout late summer and fall of 1862, various attempts by land and water were made against the city. At one time Federal gunboats had virtually confined Confederate control of the Mississippi to four miles in front of the city. But by the Southern use of the single ironclad ram *Arkansas* and other threats, the Federals were forced back for several hundred miles. It was obvious that any campaign against Vicksburg would be prolonged.

Now came Grant's role and what may be called the Second Vicksburg campaign. Vicksburg was his main goal of the winter, spring, and early summer of 1863. Seven times against the city, as the saying goes. There were the overland attempts frustrated by Earl Van Dorn's Holly Springs raid and Nathan Bedford Forrest's railroad exploits in northern Mississippi and Tennessee in December, 1862; William T. Sherman's abortive attempt at Walnut Hills and Chickasaw Bayou, also in December (often erroneously termed Chickasaw Bluffs); the Yazoo Pass expedition; the Lake Providence route west of the Mississippi; the Steele's Bayou fiasco; the Duckport and Williams's canal routes. These seven failures led to the last try. Grant wrote in his *Memoirs* that these were not serious attempts to take Vicksburg, but were mainly movements to keep his army busy![17] Grant's view has been repeated

16. *Memoirs*, I, 358; Catton, *Grant Moves South*, 251–54.
17. *Memoirs*, I, 443–44.

for years. Is it correct? I feel not. By reexamining the correspondence of the time, one gets an entirely different impression. Grant was deadly serious. The efforts were strenuous. Correspondence of other officers certainly shows that they did not take this as an exercise. Value, too, can be gained by looking at the enemy viewpoint of these thrusts. John C. Pemberton and his Confederates took them for what they really were: probing operations in force designed to capture the city of Vicksburg.

Grant deserves credit for these attempts, unsuccessful though they were. Here he demonstrated perhaps his most important trait. At Vicksburg, in a major and very lengthy campaign, he kept the pressure on. He was tenacity personified. While differing in its pressure from the later 1864–65 campaign in Virginia, Grant's strategy kept the Confederates guessing in a broad area around Vicksburg. Where would he strike next? Rumors circulated the Confederate command system of Federal attacks that never were even thought of. Grant was not beyond planting a few of these himself. This was particularly true in his final move when he sent most of his troops south of Vicksburg, across the Mississippi to come at the city from the south and finally the east. Sherman was temporarily left behind to feint at Walnut Hills and even to go into the city if he could. Benjamin H. Grierson's cavalry raid had looked like a major attacking force. Also, Vicksburg's defender Pemberton feared another field army was coming down from northern Mississippi, when in reality there was no such force.

I feel Grant deserves great credit for the Vicksburg campaign, for its many brilliant operations. He has generally received that credit. I also feel historians have missed the major point, which Grant himself missed: he put and kept the pressure on, not only at Vicksburg but in the entire Confederate Mississippi valley sector, using both real operations and feints to near perfection. Countless times this dissipated Pemberton's troops in various directions, and in the long run severely weakened him.

Then, too, I must add my voice to those who have recently questioned the broad, dramatic, and all-too-glittering generality that after crossing the Mississippi south of Vicksburg Grant cut loose from *all* supply lines, took nothing with him, and lived entirely off the country. Again, the records belie this in part. Of course he used supplies from the area, of course his army traveled light, but he did take goodly quantities of bread, other foodstuffs and ammunition as he moved inland. As soon as possible, wagons followed to keep the army supplied, and communications with the outside world, while disrupted for a time, were set up. Grant never intended to just disappear into the darkness of Mississippi. Even Vicksburg, worked over though it has been, needs even further reexamination as to Grant's role so that we can see him more in depth for today.

After the strategically momentous surrender of Vicksburg, there does come something of a lull, punctuated by the unfortunate accident in New Orleans when Grant, a superb rider, was thrown from his horse and was seriously injured. As I have stated, evidence seems to confirm that Grant was drinking in this relaxed time.[18] By mid-October he was in command of the entire Western theater of the war. In late September William Starke Rosecrans was bottled up in Chattanooga after his stunning defeat by the Confederates at Chickamauga.

Lincoln, Secretary of War Edwin M. Stanton, and the War Department urged a command change in the Army of the Cumberland. Grant, still crippled, came north to Louisville and then ordered George H. Thomas, whose performance at Chickamauga still echoes, to replace Rosecrans as commander of the Army of the Cumberland. Grant hobbled on to Chattanooga, not an easy task, due to the besieging Confederates. Two corps were brought from the east in a strikingly efficient logistical movement by rail. Sherman was brought over from the Mississippi. Grant ordered the resupplying of Chattanooga via Brown's Ferry in what became the "Cracker Line" on the Tennessee. A new attitude, businesslike and confident, seemed to prevail.

Then came the battle of Missionary Ridge. Grant, with forces of Joseph Hooker, Sherman, and especially Thomas, broke out of the Confederate encirclement and pushed Braxton Bragg's Confederates well back into Georgia. Many have read the story, repeated *ad nauseum,* of how, on November 25, 1863, after Hooker on the right and Sherman on the left seemed stalled in their attempt to force the Confederates off Missionary Ridge, Thomas's men finally got going. Grant and Thomas watched the troops go forward, supposedly to take only the outer entrenchments of the enemy, at the first low slopes of the ridge. Then, as the story goes, after the army took the lower entrenchments, every man of the thousands simultaneously got the same idea, and, without orders and to the consternation of their commanders, charged on up the near-cliff and overran the Confederate lines, beating the Confederates to a pulp.

A very nice story, except that in large part it now appears incorrect. Here is a perfect example, I feel, of the need for the historian to go back over old, familiar tales, risk the charge of rehash, but at the same time checkout just how accurate historians have been. We performed both a checkout and a checkup in our research for Bruce Catton. In his last books he pretty well demolished the legend of the unordered charge up Missionary Ridge. It took no great find from a moldy archive. It required a careful reading and rereading and new piecing together of all the messages and reports in the *Official Records* and some scattered manuscripts. What comes out clearly is not an unordered charge, but some confusion over orders, in which the majority of officers ordered the troops to go as far as they could. That some initiative was shown by these officers and their men there is no doubt, but

18. See footnote 5.

that the average soldier took it unto himself to charge on en masse is a gross exaggeration. This view does Grant, Thomas, and others a disservice. They planned well and carried out with skill the breakout from Chattanooga. They deserve the credit.[19]

Many writers tend to skip all too rapidly from Missionary Ridge clear through the winter of 1863-64 to the Virginia campaign with Grant as general in chief. This neglects his trip to Knoxville, his administration at Nashville, and his concern over east Tennessee and other places in the West such as Mobile and Georgia. We do have to skip, too, but I think a rounded picture of Grant for our time must include these trips, the strategic planning, the organizational work. Again, I wish to emphasize that all through 1863 Grant shows up more and more as a great organizer of war, a side of his genius too often submerged because of the more spectacular events he engineered.

I feel strongly that Lincoln recognized this ability when he ordered Grant east to take command of all the armies and to direct the total war strategy. Lincoln needed a general who could fight, but, even more, one who could coordinate.

Thus we have Grant's appointment first as lieutenant general and then as general in chief in March, 1864. Lincoln found his general, as it has been written. How can this be? It is a discredit both to Lincoln and to Grant. Lincoln had intensely scrutinized his available generals for a long time. Grant was not lost to Lincoln's view and therefore he did not have to be "found." Lincoln chose the only possible, the obvious candidate to bring to a successful close the enlarged and constantly growing war. Grant was the best known "lost" general in history. His capabilities and achievements were so self-evident that Lincoln could have chosen no other.

We come now to that final year of the Civil War in the East, where, beginning in early May, 1864, the Army of the Potomac pressed on against Lee day after day, in the Wilderness, at Spotsylvania, on the North Anna, at Cold Harbor, across the James, in the attacks on Petersburg, in the siege of Petersburg, on the extension of the lines, and then in the final Appomattox campaign of April, 1865. There are several points I wish to make about our protagonist in 1864 and 1865:

1. Perhaps the most important point in the 1864 campaign, perhaps the action most to Grant's credit as a soldier was the way in which the great Army of Northern Virginia was finally brought to its knees. It can be seen by observing the forces day by day. On May 4, 1864, Grant, George Gordon Meade, and the Army of the Potomac took hold of R. E. Lee and the Army of

---

19. For the charge at Missionary Ridge, see E. B. Long, "Research Notes," Fall, 1863, Chattanooga Sections I and II; Catton, *Grant Takes Command*, 79-87; *O.R.*, I, xxxi, part 2, *passim*, and particularly 132, 257-58, 264, 281, 301, 459, 512-13, 528.

Northern Virginia and held them by the throat for eleven long months! Not one hour of all that time was Lee free from the pressure. No longer could he fight a battle, rest, and then launch out on some daring exploit of his own, such as from the Peninsula to Second Manassas, into Maryland, and to Antietam in 1862; such as the Chancellorsville and Gettysburg campaigns of 1863; or the neglected Bristoe campaign of fall, 1863.

Lee was one of the most offensive-minded defensive generals in history. By 1864, everyone expected he would continue this strategy. In the Bristoe campaign in October, 1863, he got close to Washington and even considered crossing the Potomac a third time, but he finally pulled back. And this campaign, part of the "Lost Six Months of the Armies in Virginia," was R. E. Lee's last strategic offensive.[20] For now he had to contend with a stoic, determined army with a commander who had learned that there was a great deal more to victorious war than battle. Never again was R. E. Lee's army to breathe freely. Grant and Meade and the men in blue were tenaciously hanging in there.

2. For long years Lincoln and Grant were both made to look almost superhuman by some of the practitioners of the halo school of writing. Lincoln, you know, said to Grant, "the war is all yours; I don't even want to know what you are going to do or how you are going to do it. I didn't do too well with directing my other generals, so I give you a blank check." And, of course, Grant followed this, never communicating with the White House, but just going about winning a war. While I am not the first to question this legend, I do feel the evidence, both direct and indirect, shows this a gross injustice to both men. How could Lincoln, politically and otherwise, suddenly wash his hands of the war? He couldn't and he didn't. It simply was not in his character. What Lincoln meant for Grant to do, he did. Grant took over the planning, devised the strategies, and didn't bother Lincoln with details. However, through the rest of the war, Lincoln *did* know what was going on, through Grant's constant telegrams, through their rather frequent personal contacts in Washington and on the field. Lincoln spent much time at City Point headquarters near Petersburg. No, Lincoln did not let go of the reins of war. He knew where his horses were going, but he did give them more slack.

3. Many Civil War writers in the past gave the capture of Confederate geography as the main Federal objective. Then came a revisionist school that said, no, armies were the true objectives, and until Yankee generals aimed at Lee and the Confederate forces, the war could not have been won. To me these are polarizations and distortions. Despite some historians, Grant did not aim just at Lee's army. It seems there were three focal points or objectives in the North's final victory: First, Lee's army, which Grant grasped and strangled as in a vise. Second, Richmond, the capital, the spiritual heart of the

20. E. B. Long, ms. of speech, "The Lost Six Months of the Armies in Virginia."

Confederacy. Holding Lee with one hand, as it were, he shifted his army in central Virginia constantly to the left, always sliding around toward Richmond. Both Lee and Richmond had to be goals. Third, and sometimes overlooked, Grant was aiming at Virginia's connection with the rest of the Confederacy. That is why he went via Petersburg, since Richmond could not be taken rapidly. That is why Grant instituted a siege, always extending his lines, trying to cut the last links of Virginia with the South. And in the end the cutting of these vital rail lines, the containing of Lee, the pressure of the battlefield, forced the Confederates out of Richmond and to Appomattox.

On June 5, 1864, two days after Cold Harbor, Grant wired Halleck, "My idea from the start has been to beat Lee's army, if possible, north of Richmond, then, after destroying his lines of communication north of the James River to transfer the army to the south side and besiege Lee in Richmond, or follow him south if he should retreat."[21] Grant here is seeing a much more total war than he is often given credit for.

4. We have seen Grant as a planner and decision-maker, maturing from his first big opportunity at Paducah. Now we see Grant who could perceive more than one objective. On the map of Virginia he had three objectives. On a national level, too, he had a plan, simple, mature, and sufficiently broad so that if one element failed, there were alternatives. He developed goals for five national operating forces. A. Grant and Meade with the Army of the Potomac in Virginia. B. Sherman with the armies of the West to continue to carve up the Confederacy by heading into Georgia. C. Farther west, E. R. S. Canby was to get going at last after Grant's favorite western objective, Mobile. D. Ben Butler with the Army of the James was to be the southern prong while Meade in Virginia was to be the northern prong. Butler was to come in toward Petersburg from below Richmond at Bermuda Hundred. E. Franz Sigel in the Shenandoah Valley was to operate in that region to further threaten Lee. Thus we see widely dispersed armies applying pressure in five directions to the weakened Confederates who could not handle all of these threats and also watch the blockade and the various Federal enclaves along the Atlantic and Gulf coasts.[22]

Three of these five ideas failed. Butler's operations were a near-comic opera disgrace which got nowhere. Sigel's and David Hunter's actions in the valley were another disgrace, though they did tie up some Southern troops. Canby never got off the ground on the Gulf Coast, and the city of Mobile did not fall until it no longer had any meaning. But Grant had two home runs: Sherman in Georgia and himself and Meade in Virginia, and these were enough. If this is not brilliant planning and implementing of planning, I don't know what is.

21. *O.R.*, I, xxxvi, part 1, 11.
22. E. B. Long research notes for Allan Nevins, Report 12, "Grant's Plan"; *O.R.*, I, xxxii, part 3, 245–46.

5. As to the implementing, it is often said Grant was a poor judge of subordinates. True, his staff had weak links. True, in the presidential years he yielded to flattery and could not understand the machinations of the men of politics or business. But he did in some vital cases handle underlings well. John A. Rawlins was his right and even left arm on the staff; Philip H. Sheridan was the only major officer brought East. Grant had enough finesse not to kick out all the primary eastern generals and say, "Go away and let us westerners handle this." And perhaps most important, he kept George Gordon Meade, who had taken over the Army of the Potomac just before Gettysburg, who obviously had great ability, quick perception, and even quicker temper. Meade had written his wife at times after Gettysburg that he might be replaced.[23] He was not replaced. He was the operating head of the army even with his boss breathing down his neck. But Grant didn't often breathe too hard. He had better sense. He used Meade properly even if Grant stayed personally with the Army of the Potomac. Their relationship and working partnership was a credit to both men. Both had to give up something, particularly Meade. But the system worked.

6. Grant the butcher is a hard myth to extinguish. Grant is often pictured as the unfeeling martinet who ruthlessly threw thousands of men into the belching death of the cannon. As far as I can see, this is a calumny of Grant that must be refuted. Yes, casualties were high in the Wilderness, at Spotsylvania, Cold Harbor, Petersburg. Grant felt the charge at Cold Harbor to have been a mistake.[24] But how else was he to do the job but by using the methods at hand? The tools included overwhelming manpower and his use of it, usually correct, probably saved lives in the long run.

Losses were tragic, but their percentages per total manpower were comparable to those of the Confederates. An attacking army almost always loses more than the defenders. Furthermore, if Grant was to grab hold of Lee and hold on, how could he do it with anything but men? Pull back his army after a fight? Give Lee more breathing time or perhaps allow him to launch out again on his own? Hardly! Such tactics had not won the war up to now. No, Grant was a soldier striving to win a war. He was not a butcher.

In referring to courage in battle, Grant told one of his doctors, during his last illness, that it was something to be cultivated, "rather than an inherent trait."[25] He told the same doctor that carnage was "a positive horror to him,

---

23. George Meade, *The Life and Letters of George Gordon Meade* (New York, 1913), II, 168, 176, and *passim*. All during late 1863 and 1864, Meade vacillated in his concern over whether he would be removed. Part of his fear was not so much because of Grant as over the uproar about his record at Gettysburg. See also Papers of George Gordon Meade, The Historical Society of Pennsylvania, 1863 and 1864; Colonel Theodore Lyman, *Meade's Headquarters 1863–1865* (Boston, 1922), 138, 167, 204.
24. *Memoirs*, II, 276–77.
25. Dr. George F. Shrady, "General Grant's Last Days," *The Century Illustrated Monthly Magazine*, LXXVI, New Series Vol. LIV (May to Oct., 1908), 284.

and could be excused to his conscience only on the score of the awful necessity of the situation. 'It was always the idea to do it with the least suffering,' said he, 'on the same principle as the performance of a severe and necessary surgical operation.' "[26]

In an interview after Grant's death, Mrs. Grant told writer Hamlin Garland, "The general never talked war matters with me at all. He wrote very little about war matters, even after the taking of Vicksburg. I don't remember that he wrote me any letter of exultation or joy. He was so sorry for the poor fellows who were opposed to him that he never could exult over any victory. He always felt relieved of course and glad that it seemed to promise to shorten the war that much but never exulted over them. . . ." Mrs. Grant related that her husband protested when she tried to tell him of her visit to a hospital at Nashville, "No, my dear, I don't want to hear anything at all about that. I don't want you to come to me with any of these tales of the hospitals or any of these petitions and messages. I have all I can bear up under outside of my home and when I come to you I want to see you and the children and talk about other matters. I want to get all the sunshine I can."[27]

With the end of the war in 1865 came the trauma of assassination, and a new president. And with it came the time to recognize the heroes of that conflict. At the head in the public mind, after Lincoln, stood Ulysses S. Grant, the mighty victor. During the war when there was talk of his running for president in 1864, he had made it clear he had no such desire. He had often resisted or accepted with obvious diffidence the plaudits of the crowd. It wasn't that he labored under a false modesty, a cringing tossing aside of the credit. Not at all. Grant was aware of his accomplishments. But his awareness was one of admirable balance. He had been successful where others had failed. He had been given a task and he had done it. He had developed tremendously as a soldier and as a person.

The hoped-for final volume of the Lloyd Lewis-Bruce Catton biography of Grant will undoubtedly give us new insights into Grant during the Andrew Johnson years, the Stanton-Johnson struggle, and the reorganization of the postwar army. At present there are places here where Grant seems to have been on unfamiliar and unstable ground and where, to me, he is not at his best.

Then came the eight years of the presidency. Reexamination of these years is certainly called for. If the traditional picture is correct, of Grant as one of our most inept presidents, to the point where he is almost a political buffoon, so be it. But if this is partially an inaccurate picture, as I suspect from my own investigations it is, we are due for some judicious and fair revisionism.

The immediate post-Civil War period in the country seems often to have

26. *Ibid.*, 107.
27. Interview with Julia Dent Grant, Garland Papers.

been studied in separate packages—the South in Reconstruction; Johnson versus the Congress; the expansion of the West; Grant, big business, and the beginning of the "Gilded Age." This results in lopsided, compartmented history, when what we need is a combination of all these subjects which existed simultaneously and have clear interrelation. Perhaps if this is done, we can get a surer balance on Grant the president.

Thus we have looked briefly at Ulysses S. Grant. It is said of Lincoln that he was an uncommon common man. I think it can be said of Grant that he was a rather common or slightly more than a common man; that he was not a man of great depth or profundity; that he had no overpowering charisma. But in the postwar period people could identify with him, war hero or not. He was like them. General John M. Schofield said that Grant probably didn't understand himself and "perhaps there was nothing special in Grant to understand."[28] He felt Grant's most extraordinary quality was his extreme simplicity, "so extreme that many have entirely overlooked it in their search for some deeply hidden secret . . . He was incapable of any attempt to deceive anybody. . . . The greatest of all the traits of Grant's character was that which lay always on the surface, visible to all who had eyes to see."[29] "Grant is the most unassuming officer I have ever seen," one member of his headquarters guard commented.[30]

His observant doctor wrote that Grant was never "openly demonstrative in any direction, he appeared the same under all conditions. When he was depressed, he was simply silent; when he was cheerful, he merely smiled. Even in his best moods I never heard him laugh outright. . . ."[31]

Grant had a certain practical ability; he could deal with facts as he found them if they were not clothed in subtleties. He had been labeled a failure in prewar days, a condition with which common men could identify. He had risen to be a great captain of men, and had been president, typifying the highest workings of the American tradition.

He will stand, possibly for centuries, as a military man of great or even surpassing ability. Possibly he always will be considered by many to have been somewhat a failure as president and businessman. Literary men, as well as historians, will no doubt continue to read, study and admire the *Memoirs*, his last triumph. Research shows quite convincingly that Grant wrote them himself, while battling terminal throat cancer, a feat of the most profound endurance. Neither secretary Adam Badeau nor his son Frederick Dent Grant

---

28. Interview with John M. Schofield, Garland Papers.
29. *Ibid.*
30. Gerhard Luke Luhn to family, undated (1864), Gerhard Luke Luhn Collection, Western History Research Center, University of Wyoming.
31. Shrady, 411.

had any major hand in the work. The pages of the *Memoirs* are his own, his last testament.[32]

Much can be learned from this man who held a center stage position in our history for well over fifteen years. Here is a man I would have liked to have known. He does not frighten one. I think we can understand Grant even through the vehicle of history, at least as much as we can understand any man. Here is a man who is receiving and deserves some new investigation, some new thought. Grant is a man whose attributes are sometimes at variance with what we think requisite for America's heroes. He fits better the pattern of the American average man who did something unaverage.

One soldier told author Hamlin Garland, "he was a man in whom the army had confidence, but they did not love him. He'd ride past without their knowing . . . a few of the army knew him by sight." But they "knew him and trusted him and he knew them. They went with him like men to a game, no despondency, all alert and eager, glad to know inaction had ended and vigorous work had begun."[33]

He did not attract the outward manifestations of love from his army as did McClellan, Lee, or Jackson. But he received something more—confidence, trust, steadiness. There was that night in the Wilderness of Virginia. The Federal Army of the Potomac had crossed the rivers as it had done before, and several times before it had fallen back. The lead troops this night came to a fork in the road. One led south from the Wilderness toward Spotsylvania and one back toward the Rapidan and the Rappahannock. In the darkness of that Wilderness, some of Winfield Scott Hancock's men spied the slouched figure of Grant, the taller thin figure of Meade, and their staffs, moving along the Brock Road. Word passed rapidly among the men: Grant's horse's head was turned toward Richmond. Weary, sleepy soldiers rushed to the roadside. Wild cheers echoed through the brush forest. As one officer put it, "The night march had become a triumphal procession for the new commander." They were not going back again, despite two days of ferocious battle. They were headed south on the road to victory. The whole Army of the Potomac seemed to take on a new life.[34]

No one ever lit up at the literary beauty of Grant's speeches. He did not pen the Gettysburg Address. Some of his short phrases hit a public chord, but they were not coined for that. The "unconditional surrender" message and his message to the Republican convention, "Let us have peace," were not

32. For Badeau and Grant, see *Battles and Leaders*, Extra Illustrated, Vol. III, clippings and letters, Huntington Library, San Marino, Calif., among other sources.
33. Interview with Judge J. H. Robinson, Garland Papers.
34. Horace Porter, *Campaigning with Grant* (New York, 1897), 78–79; Harold Adams Small, ed., *The Road to Richmond: The Civil War Memoirs of Maj. Abner R. Small of the 16th Maine Vols. . . .* (Berkeley, 1957), 134; James Harrison Wilson, *The Life of John A. Rawlins* (New York, 1916), 215.

calculated slogans. But the public picked them up. They were part of that confidence people had in him. They seemed to know what to expect from General Grant. There were few surprises.

He was not an intellectual; he was not a man of culture. He was a bourgeois man. One of the doctors who attended his final illness quoted Grant as saying of himself that he "was a mere workingman on the field" who believed "What was to be, would be, . . . It was to have been."[35] This same doctor wrote, "His was a Christianity that taught him to submit to whatever might come. Religion supported him on one side, and philosophy on the other."[36]

And yet, for all the points we have discussed, and for many others we might consider, I wonder if Grant himself, with that unintentional economy of language, did not sum himself up when he wrote out in shaky handwriting, no longer able to speak because of the cancer in his throat. "A verb is anything that signifies to be; to do; or to suffer. I signify all three."[37]

---

35. Shrady, 276.
36. *Ibid.*, 275.
37. Grant to Dr. John H. Douglas, undated (1885), facsimile in Horace Green, *General Grant's Last Stand* (New York, 1936), 47.

III

"We Sail Directly for the Isthmus"[1]

By Charles G. Ellington

At 2:00 P.M., on July 5, 1852, eight companies of the 4th Infantry with the band and headquarters departed from Governors Island, New York, for the Isthmus of Panama on the steamship *Ohio*. The oaken side-wheeler was built in New York to carry 330 passengers on three decks in comfort. Her flying-serpent's figurehead and extended bowsprit gave the *Ohio* a sprightly look.[2]

The *Ohio* had been on the New York-Panama run since the fall of 1849. For an earlier voyage, the *New York Commercial Advertiser* had reported that "The steam ship Ohio leaves this afternoon at 3 o'clock for Navy Bay, with five hundred and fifty passengers for California." *The Shipping and Commercial List, and New-York Price Current* also advertised the sailing: "the splendid double engine steam ship OHIO, (3000 tons burthen,) J. F. Schenck, U.S.N., Commander, will sail . . . direct for CHAGRES, connecting . . . for San Francisco on arrival of the passengers and mails at Panama."[3] The passengers on this trip of the *Ohio* were the last ever landed at Chagres by the big steamers; after November, 1851, steamship lines disembarked their passengers at Aspinwall.

During the voyage, Lieutenant J. Finley Schenck captained the *Ohio*, and fifty-six-year-old Lieutenant Colonel Benjamin Louis Eulalie de Bonneville led the military. The 4th Infantry had been commanded by Colonel William Whistler of Maryland, an army regular now too ancient for field service, who

1. The title of this chapter is the opening sentence of a letter of July 5, 1852, from Ulysses S. Grant to his wife, Julia Dent Grant, on the day he sailed for the Pacific Coast. John Y. Simon, ed., *The Papers of Ulysses S. Grant* (Carbondale and Edwardsville, Ill., 1967-), I, 247 (hereafter cited as *PUSG*).
2. John Haskell Kemble, *The Panama Route* (Berkeley, 1943), 239.
3. Newspapers cited in Georgia Willis Read, "The Chagres River Route to California in 1851," *Quarterly of the California Historical Society*, VIII (March, 1929), 7.

was placed on indefinite leave of absence.[4] Ulysses S. Grant, the senior first lieutenant in the 4th Infantry and brevet captain, was the regimental quartermaster, a position of recognized responsibility.

The trip was uncomfortable from the start. The ship was terribly crowded since the 651 military men, and over 50 of their family members, were pushed onto the steamer already loaded with men on their way to the goldfields of California. Grant counted more than 1,100 souls on board. Moreover, they sailed amid upsetting reports to the senior medical officer, Major Charles Stuart Tripler, that a cholera epidemic was in full swing on the Isthmus. His wife, Eunice, who thought Bonneville "a very stupid man mentally," did not accompany her husband to California, but she recorded his distress: "Dr. Tripler thought it a great cruelty to start them at a season when cholera was raging on the Isthmus . . . Before leaving New York, [he] wrote the Surgeon General it was murder to attempt the crossing of the Isthmus then. But the reply was it would be 'quickly over.' "[5] The army was about to make a serious mistake.

Fortunately, the climate was delightful during the voyage from New York to their destination, Aspinwall. Grant wrote that "We have been blessed with remarkably fine weather from the begining . . ."[6] Every evening the military band played and the passengers danced. The passengers got acquainted by cardplaying, fishing, spotting whales, and easy conversation about what lay ahead. But with little room for exercise in cramped quarters and the temperature rising each day, inactivity and boredom took their toll. Sometimes, according to Grant, the cabins were "so insufferably hot that no one can stay there."[7] And, the young captain, who later traveled the world's sealanes with never a stomach quiver, was among those who became seasick.

Sam Grant was popular among his fellow officers. Those who had served with him in Mexico especially respected him and held him in high esteem. Second Lieutenant Henry C. Hodges met Grant for the first time just before sailing. Hodges described him as "a thin, quiet, reticent man, full of kindly and generous feeling for those about him."[8]

Although Grant had the reputation of being a professional and "giving close and strict attention to his duties,"[9] Bonneville, at first, wanted to have another quartermaster. Perhaps this was because Grant had a reputation of being Whistler's man or for some other unknown reason. There was opposi-

4. Col. William Whistler nominally commanded the 4th Infantry from July, 1845, until he retired Oct., 1861. Grant served under him at Detroit and Sackets Harbor, N.Y., 1849–52.
5. Louis A. Arthur, ed., Eunice Tripler; Some Notes of Her Personal Recollections (New York, 1910), 106–8.
6. PUSG, I, 248.
7. Ibid.
8. Henry C. Hodges to William C. Church, Jan. 7, 1897, William C. Church Papers, Library of Congress.
9. Ibid.

tion on the part of other 4th Infantry officers to making a change, however, and, since Bonneville did not care that much, the matter was dropped. The fact was that Captain Grant preferred Whistler as his commanding officer rather than Bonneville. Even after arriving on the West Coast, Grant wrote to Julia: "We are somewhat in hope that Col. Whistler will join us here. He writes that he is determined to come . . ."[10]

Years later, the *Ohio*'s master would recall the trip to Panama and Sam Grant. Schenck thought Grant a very quiet person who took the world as he found it, but who could be counted upon to have opinions and to back them up. The *Ohio*'s captain did not like Bonneville, thought him hasty and uncertain in his actions, always being bailed out by his sensible quartermaster. As the ship steamed southward the navy captain and the sleepless young army captain would walk up and down the deck at night talking of many things and becoming better acquainted. Schenck found Grant an educated, intelligent man, and one whose mind took hold of ideas, grasped them strongly, and digested them thoroughly.[11]

Another passenger aboard the *Ohio* remembered the day that some of the officers were having a difference of opinion on the main deck, while Grant sat by himself on the opposite side, out of hearing. As the argument got warmer, and the prospect of agreement less, the regimental adjutant suggested: "I tell you, fellows, how we will settle this. Let's go across the deck and refer the whole matter to long-headed Sam, and whatever may be his decision we will abide by it." This was not the only dispute during that boring trip that "long-headed Sam" was called upon to mediate.[12]

One source of amusement which helped pass the time was the group's careful observation of the new commander, who was definitely a "character." Bonneville, an old frontiersman, was a small man, deliberate and very much the dandy. He carried a cane and wore a large, white, stiff beaver hat to cover his bald dome. His sense of dignity and his hat never deserted him all the miles from New York Harbor to the shores of the broad Columbia.

Certain junior members of the 4th, allied with well-hidden sailors, would shout with great irreverence, "Where did you get that hat?" as Bonneville stomped around the deck each day. Try as he might the old warrior could not catch a single one of these pesky jokers, adding to the general merriment of the bored passengers. One observer thought Bonneville "a most gallant and experienced officer, [but with] a somewhat arbitrary and testy temper."[13]

10. *PUSG*, I, 287.
11. Interview in *New York Herald*, n.d., cited in Hamlin Garland, "Grant's Quiet Years at Northern Posts," *McClure's Magazine*, VIII (March, 1897), 406–7.
12. William Conant Church, *Ulysses S. Grant . . .* (New York, 1897), 50.
13. William S. Lewis, ed., *Reminiscences of Delia B. Sheffield* (Seattle, 1924), 5 (hereafter cited as Lewis, *Sheffield*).

Anticipation was high, however, and a crusty commanding officer was not that unusual.

Bonneville was born in Paris in 1796 and graduated from West Point in 1815. In the early 1830s, on leave from the army, he led a three-year trapping expedition through the Rocky Mountains that brought him considerable publicity. It was the first major exploration since the Lewis and Clark expedition and took Bonneville down the Columbia River into Hudson's Bay territory. He never reached one of his objectives, Fort Vancouver, but won a reputation with a great assist from the well-known author, Washington Irving, who upon Bonneville's return, edited and published the trip's journal as the *Adventures of Captain Bonneville, U.S.A.* . . . . Although criticized for some commercial aspects of his exploration, he was recognized as a frontier leader.

As the ship plowed on, Grant was already experiencing the lonely forces that later engulfed him. Trying to see the bright side, he noted to Julia that his expectations were high for "this move. I expect by it to do something for myself."[14] But, loner that he was, Grant spent his hours walking back and forth, head down and deep in thought. One young passenger noted during every day and every evening he spent his time "pacing the deck and smoking, silent and solitary." She noticed also that he smoked too much. Fellow passengers considered Sam Grant a thoughtful and serious officer, not given to light talk, but "affable in manner." When old Bonneville became arbitrary and difficult, it was the quartermaster who helped to smooth over the unpleasantness.[15]

The inactivity of the voyage ended on July 16 when the *Ohio* reached Aspinwall (later renamed Colón) in Limon Bay, starting point for the Isthmus crossing. The town, named after the Pacific Mail Steamship Company's first president and a founder of the Panama Railroad Company, was built on a marshy island from earth and rock brought back from the railroad construction site. The fill was dumped in a swamp which had been described as stinking and unbearable with a generous population of sand-flies, mosquitoes, snakes, and venomous insects.

William Henry Aspinwall was senior partner in the largest New York export-import firm of the day, Howland and Aspinwall. The company traded extensively in Europe and the Far East, and was beginning to do business with Hispanic America. Aspinwall, a wealthy man, was considered one of the soundest merchants in New York. Of all the builders of the Panama-Pacific route, "Aspinwall stands out, not only as the ablest leader and most commanding personality, but also as a man of admirable character."[16]

Aspinwall during the rainy season was a mess. The unpaved streets were

14. *PUSG*, I, 249.
15. Lewis, *Sheffield*, 5–6.
16. Kemble, *Panama Route*, 23.

Fig. 1. THE ISTHMUS OF PANAMA.
Map drawn by J. A. Lloyd and published by J. Oakes, New York City, in 1849.
Reproduced from the original in the Henry E. Huntington Library. The author has
modified the map in order to highlight the crossing of the 4th Infantry Regiment in
July, 1852.

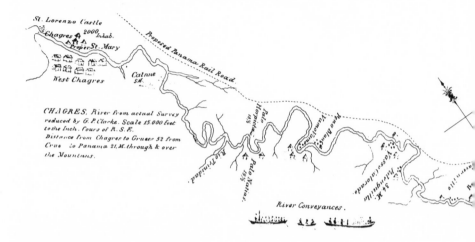

Fig. 2. MAP OF THE CHAGRES ROUTE.
"View of Chagres, Lorenzo Castle, Indian Village of Chagres; Correct Map of Chagres River; with distances, West Chagres or American Side. Taken on the Spot June 16th 1850 by George P. Clarke."
Map published in 1850 by Stringer & Townsend, New York City. Reproduced from the Book Club of California's 1965 series, John Haskell Kemble, ed., *The Panama Canal: The Evolution of the Isthmus Crossing*.

Fig. 3. THE OLD LAS CRUCES-PANAMA TRAIL, 1914.
"The trail was already more than 200 years old when Grant used it. Not all of it was paved as well as this section and there were holes in it 4 and 5 feet deep," writes R. Z. Kirkpatrick in "General Grant in Panama," *The Military Engineer,* XXVI, 146 (March–April, 1934), 131.
Photograph reprinted with the permission of The Society of American Military Engineers.

Fig. 4. THE VILLAGE OF CRUCES, 1912.
Cruces was destroyed by the filling of Gatun Lake. This photograph was taken shortly before the destruction of the village, and it had changed little since Grant had been there.

Fig. 5. A Mexican-Indian Hut between Gorgona and Panama.
Illustration of a resting place on the Gorgona trail to Panama City by Gilbert Gaul after a drawing by Charles Nahl in 1850.
It appeared in an article "To California by Panama in '49" in *The Century Magazine,* April, 1891.

Fig. 6. View of the Isthmus Crossing in December, 1854.
Dr. Fessenden N. Otis, a United States Mail Steamship Company surgeon, drew this sketch of the Summit at Culebra in December, 1854. This was as far as the railroad went at the time, with Culebra being about ten miles short of Panama City and thirty-seven miles from the Atlantic.
The sketch was lithographed by C. Parson and printed by Endicott & Co., New York City, in 1854.
Reproduced from the Book Club of California's 1965 series, John Haskell Kemble, ed., *The Panama Canal: The Evolution of the Isthmus Crossing.*

deep in water with make-shift, raised planks providing "sidewalks." Grant wondered how anybody could live there and why anybody would want to. But the town flourished with a mixture of American and Spanish culture; it even had its own English-language newspaper. Aspinwall was the Atlantic terminus for the "Panama Route" which became the premier link between the United States' two coastal areas. The overland passage, with its well-known difficulties, and the long trip "round the horn" could not compete with the Panama route for speed or dependability. Between 1848 and 1869 thousands of travelers and tons of merchandise jostled between Chagres or Aspinwall on the Atlantic, and Panama City on the Pacific. A loose but organized network of small paddle-wheelers, native canoes, mule trains, and, finally, the railroad, became an integral part of America's transportation system. Until the golden spike riveted the nation together in 1869, "the ordinary person or message could not travel between the Atlantic and Pacific Coasts more swiftly or surely than by way of Panama."[17]

When it was first discovered in 1501 the Isthmus was called Darien, which for years was used synonymously with Panama. Just a few degrees north of the equator, the Isthmus is so narrow that you can see both oceans from several low peaks. Only one mountain in the vicinity of the crossing has an elevation over 3,000 feet; most are under 650 feet. The geography is a bit confusing. The Isthmus is east of Florida, and lies generally east and west: thus, to reach the Pacific from the Atlantic the traveler went south.

Many rivers rise in the mountains, but only one is identified forever with the affairs of that region. Christopher Columbus named it Rio Lagartos, River of Alligators; Balboa called it the Chagres. Henry Morgan the pirate was there, as was Francis Drake and a host of conquistadors and adventurers. Originally it was the Spanish river gateway to the wealth of the Incas and one author believed: "The Chagres is the world's most valuable river."[18]

The Chagres, today mostly submerged by Canal Zone lakes, was about 120 miles long and several hundred feet wide. Depending on the season, the river could be five feet deep for miles, with some places twenty-five feet in depth. During the frequent flash floods the river could rise forty feet in a single day. The Chagres usually flowed steadily, curving in and out, with some shoals and rapids, bordered by heavily-jungled banks all the way from Cruces down to the Caribbean. The river was the dominant physical and historical feature of the Isthmus, and the California-bound travelers were impressed.

Panama's climate is even, month in and month out. Early morning temperatures are a pleasant 72–74 degrees; by mid-day, they are up to 84–90 degrees. The wet "winter season" is from June to November and the dry season is usually January to April (December and May are considered

17. *Ibid.*, vi, and author's interview with Dr. Kemble.
18. John Easter Minter, *The Chagres* . . . (New York, 1948), 5.

intermediary months). It rains every month of the year; annual rainfall is as high as twelve feet on the Atlantic side and half of that on the Pacific.

The Panama Railroad, the marvel of its day, was pushed through the jungles and over the rivers by thousands of workers and, after a struggle of almost five years, completed in February, 1855. One historian wrote: "I look upon the construction of the Panama Railroad . . . as being as great, if not greater, an undertaking as the building of the canal . . . This was the first transcontinental railroad in the world."[19]

By 1855, the ocean-to-ocean Isthmus crossing could be made in less than a day. Said to be the most expensive stretch of track ever built, the Panama Railroad was also the most profitable. Reputable sources claimed it was the "perfect monopoly," earning six million dollars in its first seven years, and was prosperous even after the "other" transcontinental railroad took away much of its traffic in 1869.[20]

But in mid-1852 when the 4th Infantry disembarked, the railroad had been completed only to Barbacoas almost twenty miles inland (five miles short of Gorgona) where a four-hundred-foot bridge over the Chagres was being constructed. The first time California-bound passengers were carried over the railroad was seven months before the 4th Infantry arrived when 700 passengers from the *Georgia* took the rails about eight miles up the line over the objections of the local railroad management. They were fearful it would interfere with the progress of the work.[21]

Upon arrival in Aspinwall, it became apparent that the 4th Infantry faced serious trouble. The Pacific Mail Steamship Company agents who had contracted to move the regiment from the Atlantic to the Pacific were not prepared for their arrival. In-transit goldseekers had bought or rented all the accommodations, inflated the price of labor and mules, and created havoc with the transport system.

To ease the problem the agent suggested that the regiment split into small parties and take two routes. At this time, the normal path to the Pacific was in three stages: the unfinished Panama Railroad to the Chagres River at Barbacoas; native boats upriver to the head of navigation (Gorgona or Cruces, depending on the season); and a mule train on into Panama City. The troops, who had expected to ride after going upriver as far as possible, were now ordered to march to Panama after reaching Gorgona.

Gorgona and Cruces were settled because they were the best spots at the head of navigation on the Chagres. Each place had "two or three respectable forwarding houses and hotels, owned by Americans."[22] Miller's Hotel, the

19. C. L. G. Anderson, *Old Panama* (New York, 1938), 10.
20. David Howarth, *Panama* . . . (New York, 1966), 185, and interview with Dr. Kemble, Aug., 1978.
21. Read, 10.
22. Chauncey D. Griswold, *The Isthmus of Panama* (New York, 1852), 46.

French Hotel, and the Spanish and American House were in Gorgona. In Cruces, the leading hostelry was Ran Runnels's American Hotel, which featured, in late 1851, supper, cot, and breakfast for two dollars. The village houses of the natives were usually "huts, made of canes and covered with long dried leaves commonly taken from palm-trees."[23] The population moved up and down with the level of the river since the commission merchants, transportation agents, and hotelkeepers switched from Gorgona to Cruces for the rainy season. Also, as many as five hundred Americans awaiting ships to San Francisco would lie over in the villages in a vain attempt to escape Panama City's high cost of living.

The baggage, the band, civilians, and those who were ill, were to take the Cruces route where a limited number of pack mules would be available. The two groups were then to meet where the routes united, about five miles above Panama. Drum-Major Elderkin told how the journey started: "We had Grant's superintendence in packing all the arms, putting forty in each sack, and then the sailors sewed them up. We had to pack them on mules across the isthmus . . . Grant staid until the stores were all started . . . [and] had to look after the health of his soldiers and the people going with him . . ."[24]

Most of the regiment, seven companies and the regimental headquarters, moved promptly by rail to the river crossing and then by native "bungo" dugouts to the town of Gorgona. The trail from Gorgona to Panama City, with all its shortcomings, was not more than twenty miles in length, crossing the Continental Divide by an easier route than the Cruces trail. In normal weather, only the first five miles or so were really bad; the rest, with certain exceptions, was unremarkable. The route, however, was good only during the dry season because it ran so close to rivers, streams, and marshland. When it rained, the clay and marshes turned into impassable mud with as many as nineteen stream crossings. At the trail's "Half-way House," two large tents had been set up to provide some protection and a rest area for traveling Americans. In July, 1852, the Gorgona trail was a morass, and the troops were unable to carry their normal equipment. Bonneville, leading the main body, slogged to the Pacific in two or three days and boarded the waiting steamship.

The regimental quartermaster was dispatched farther upriver to Cruces, with one company as escort, carrying camp and garrison equipment, tents, mess chests, kettles, supervising soldiers, their wives and children, and miscellaneous civilians. This initiated a harrowing trip long remembered.

Starting off, Grant's group included: Dr. Tripler; Brevet Major and Mrs. John H. Gore, old and dear friends from Detroit and Sackets Harbor, New York, with their little son; Brevet Captain Henry Davis Wallen, 2nd, com-

23. E. L. Autenrieth, *Isthmus of Panama* (New York, 1851), 9, 14; Read, 13.
24. Interview with Drum-Major Elderkin, Hamlin Garland Papers, University of Southern California Library, Los Angeles (hereafter cited as Garland-Elderkin interview).

manding the escort company, his wife Anne, sons Harry and Eddy, and daughter Nann; Second Lieutenant John Withers, commanding the guard; the wives of Second Lieutenants Slaughter, Collins, and Underwood; Elijah Camp and Mr. Alford; Sergeant D. G. Sheffield and his sixteen-year-old bride, Delia; Drum-Major Elderkin and his young wife; Mr. and Mrs. Lynch with three small children; wives of enlisted men, including Mrs. Kelley and Margaret Getz, who had been Julia Grant's household helper; and a small contingent of Catholic Sisters of Charity, who had joined the group. Grant's bungo boat journey with this diverse company was not without incident and thoroughly unpleasant.

He later recalled that the "boats carried thirty to forty passengers each. The crews consisted of six men to a boat, armed with long poles . . . [and] not inconveniently burdened with clothing." Top speed as they poled along was "a mile to a mile and a half an hour . . . against the current of the river."[25]

Delia Sheffield never forgot the trip up the Chagres in those boats. Years later she wrote of the "strong and swift current" which made progress so slow. When night came the boats were tied to the bank while the natives "went up to a little village [where] they caroused all night . . . while we sat in shivering terror in the boats, kept awake by their shouting and fearing an attack from the drunken barbarians." When at last the long night was over, the journey was resumed only to see knife fights break out among the boat crews "which greatly frightened the women and children of the party." Delia praised Captain Grant who "in his quiet unassuming manner seemed to provide for everyone and we all had the highest praise for him."[26]

Wallen recalled that while he and Grant were moving up the Chagres a "report came back that a boat had capsized and those on board had been drowned." But the report proved false, and after they determined that all the army wives were safe, the trip upriver continued.[27]

Grant got his party safely to Cruces, which was five miles or so above Gorgona, but found Edmund Duckworth, the contractor, could produce neither animals nor native porters. "There was not a mule . . . in the place," Grant noted.[28] The town was a lively spot, crowded with natives and travelers moving down the streets at all hours. The noise made sleep almost impossible. Cruces had a church and Gorgona had "a place they call by that name, though to me it looked like anything but a church," observed one American.[29] Both villages had taverns, ample whiskey, and more than a few whores.

It was a trying time at Cruces that summer of 1852 with terrible weather,

25. *Personal Memoirs of U. S. Grant* (New York, 1885–86), I, 195 (hereafter cited as *Memoirs*).
26. Lewis, *Sheffield*, 6–7.
27. Frank A. Burr, *Life of General Grant* (Philadelphia, 1885), 113.
28. *Memoirs*, I, 196.
29. *Journal of Henry Sturdivant from December 8, 1849, of Cumberland, Maine*, Henry E. Huntington Library, San Marino, Calif., 7.

cholera, and inadequate shelter. The situation worsened as the baggage was exposed to heavy rains and became soggy, making large amounts of it unusable. Several of the party guarding the equipment died of cholera. To minimize the risk and make progress, Captain Sam sent the escort company on to Panama City and stayed behind to organize those left. Now with Grant, to look after the women and the sick, were Lieutenant Withers's shrinking guard force and Dr. Tripler. Grant remained until everyone started "on mules or in litters . . . excepting one or two who were so low with the cholera that they could not be carried. . . . These persons were removed to comfortable quarters, the services of a Doctor employed and arrangements made for their transmission through to Panama as soon as they should recover sufficiently."[30] Grant recalled that "I was left alone with the sick and the soldiers who had families."[31] Drum-Major Elderkin reminisced:

[Grant] was afraid [my wife and I] would take the cholera; he took great interest in us, and told me that I had better start and go to Panama, and he gave me twenty dollars and said . . . If you cannot get a mule, you had better start off alone. Your wife cannot go with skirts on. So I put onto my wife a pair of my white pantaloons, and a white shirt . . . I told Captain Grant that I had everything but a coat, and he said, I have one that will just fit her, and he went to his trunk and took out one, and then she put on my sword belt. He said, you buy some claret wine, and don't drink any water while you are on the way . . . When we got near Panama we met the American Counsel coming out on a horse, and he said, the cholera is in Panama . . . [32]

Cholera, a gastrointestinal disease, is caused by a bacillus that lodges in the intestinal tract and is spread by food and water contaminated by human excrement. This dreaded and infectious disease is bred of poor sanitation and passed along by drinking, or washing in, water containing human fecal matter, or from eating fruits or vegetables contaminated by such matter, or from food prepared by unclean hands. The disease would incubate in the body for five days before symptoms appeared. Quick death from cholera resulted from massive loss of body fluid, as much as several gallons a day through diarrhea and vomiting, and shock brought about by the sudden imbalance of body chemicals. A hard-hit victim can die in a matter of hours. In its classic form of the 1800s, "cholera vibrio" killed about one-half of its victims.[33]

After waiting impatiently for three days, Grant set out to hire men and mules on his own and to move the remaining Americans to Panama City. He

30. *PUSG*, I, 270–71.
31. *Memoirs*, I, 197.
32. Garland-Elderkin interview. There are several versions of the Elderkin interview in Garland's papers. The author has used Garland's notes made after he talked with the old drum-major in Detroit in 1896.
33. This description of cholera comes from three sources: Don Schaneke, *Los Angeles Times*, Sept. 25, 1977; *Time* and *Newsweek*, both dated Sept. 26, 1977.

was exhibiting already the characteristics noted later by a grateful wartime president when he said of Grant, "Wherever he is, things move!" On July 21, 1852, army records show that Captain Sam contracted with José Ma. Saravia for the animals "at more than double the original price."[34]

Captain Wallen recalled that: "Grant in his capacity as quartermaster immediately perfected arrangements for sending [the ladies] across the Isthmus. This had to be done on hammocks thrown on the shoulders of [native] men with relays provided at convenient distances along the two days' journey" from Cruces to Panama City.[35]

Years later, Hodges wrote that "the most laborious part [of the entire trip] fell to the lot of our quartermaster, Captain Grant [whose] services were of the greatest importance and were highly creditable to himself and the regiment. His kindness and thoughtfulness were not confined to his own command, but he assisted many [civilian] passengers in getting across the Isthmus."[36]

The mule trip from Cruces to the Pacific Coast was usually two days, but Grant's party thought it would go on forever. It was even worse than the canoe journey. Only about twenty miles or so long, the "all weather road" from the north end of Cruces to Panama City was not worthy of the name. Rough, narrow, and hazardous, it was pocked with holes and coated with mud, but had a foundation of cobblestones. The Cruces route followed generally the ancient Spanish Trail connecting Panama with Porto Bello. A more northerly route which avoided marshlands, it had actually been "paved" centuries before and there was enough stonework remaining to give the mules some measure of footing. A modern writer noted that although this mule trip was over historic ground, few knew it and nobody cared.[37] A traveler of 1851 thought the Cruces trail was a "gutter of mud between rocks on a shelf at the top of a precipice."[38]

This more northerly Cruces trail avoided most of the streams, but it was more rugged than the Gorgona road, crossing a number of hilly spurs and zigzagging through ravines. One military traveler said traversing these spurs was like "a succession of stairs, up and down, with a hole in each step about three inches deep worn by the feet of the animals . . . into which your horse or mule inserts his foot, and you cannot make him place it anywhere else."[39] A knowledgeable Panama resident called it "certainly the worst and most fatiguing road we ever traveled."[40]

34. Memoirs, I, 198; PUSG, I, 249-50.
35. Burr, Grant, 113.
36. Hodges as cited in note 8.
37. Howarth, Panama, 174.
38. Oscar Lewis, Sea Routes to the Gold Fields (New York, 1949), 182. Lewis writes that Henry Sturdivant was this traveler, but the author's study of Sturdivant's Journal does not confirm this.
39. Roland Dennis Hussey, Spanish Colonial Trails in Panama (Mexico, 1939), 60.
40. Autenrieth, Isthmus, 12.

There were no high mountains in this sector but a large number of gullies which were loosely connected to form the "highway." With the passage of years and thousands of hooves, the gullies became deeper and deeper, always narrowing at the bottom. Most were so tight that one-way traffic was a necessity. Although the natives whooped and hollered when entering a gully, two parties would inevitably meet in the middle, and arguments about who had to back up were loud, long, and sometimes violent.

A few months before Grant passed, George Willis Reed noted the pleasant, dense forest shading the beginning of the Cruces route, but in a few miles changed his mind. "*Road* did I call this miserable attempt at a footpath? . . . However, we drove on against rocks, ditches, mudholes . . . covered with mud, worn out and sorely depressed in spirits . . ."[41]

The scenery was exotic, with tropical beauty all around. A tangled jungle of green, coconut trees, tropical ferns, and vivid orange and scarlet flowers was there for the travelers to view. Monkeys chattered, parrots kept up an incessant screeching, wild turkeys sat in the treetops, pheasants and pigeons flew in large numbers, but single-file, plodding along the muddy mule-track, Grant's group had no eye for the splendor of the scene. The ladies rode or walked or were carried in hammocks; there was little agreement as to which method of torture was the worst. A few of the women who walked almost fainted from the heat and ended up with raw and bleeding feet. Grant recorded that Anne Wallen arrived in Panama weighing eighty-four pounds, suffering a substantial loss.

Attractive, clear springs were seen beside the trail at decent intervals, but Captain Grant "warned [the party] against drinking any of the water . . . as he said it would cause fever."[42] Speed was limited by three factors: the animal's inclination, the traveler's seat, and the trail itself, which was "almost without bottom."[43] Along with pots, kettles, and other equipment, Grant had to transport the mountain of knapsacks the soldiers could not carry over the foot trail from Gorgona to Panama.

As members of Grant's party became ill they would slide off the backs of the mules, but the indifferent natives would toss them back up to continue the jolting ride. The mules, small but sturdy, were bearing loads out of all proportion to their size, so they too became weary as the trip went on. One of the Catholic Sisters contracted cholera at Cruces, but Grant was able to keep her in a hammock all the way to Panama.

Captain Sam watched Henry Wallen's children struggling to keep up and never doubted that his decision to leave pregnant Julia and his infant son, Fred, behind, was the right one. Every child Fred's age or younger, and there

41. Read, 13.
42. Lewis, *Sheffield*, 8.
43. Church, *Grant*, 49.

were twenty of them, either died on the crossing or shortly thereafter.[44] "My dearest," he wrote, "you never could have crossed the Isthmus at this season . . ."[45] Grant did not know that Ulysses S. Grant, Jr., had been born as he prepared to move down the Cruces trail.

Near exhaustion, half-dead with fatigue, tired and unkempt from exposure to heat and rain, the travelers continued on. The women and children who made this hard and weary trip remembered, all their lives, the kindness and self-sacrifice of the officers who helped them walk across the Isthmus in 1852. And, Ulysses S. Grant was remembered most.[46]

The explorer Lionel Gisborne, going in the opposite direction, passed Captain Sam's party on the Cruces trail. He noted that there were not enough mules for the army wives and that: "Modesty gave way to necessity; some had most wisely put on trowsers, and discarded the petticoat, but most of them tucked this feminine garment to above the knee, and tramped along through mud and over rocks with greater spirit than the men."[47]

Just before reaching Panama City the Cruces and Gorgona routes joined at Cruz de Cardenas where there were several houses and one last river to cross. But now the trail flattened out, several smaller avenues from both north and south joined in, and the road became a highway. Farms were seen on both sides; carts hauling produce, water-carriers, and miscellaneous travelers all joined the pack mule parade. Saddle-sore, tired and dirty, the swaying, three-day ride came to an end and Grant's straggling, wet party first viewed the Pacific Ocean on July 25 or 26. Grant summed up: "The horrors of the road, in the rainy season, are beyond description."[48]

Now closed up, the 4th Infantry found Panama filled with frustrated and impatient men, brothels, saloons, and gambling dens. Temporary camps had grown up on the outskirts of town and it was here that malaria, yellow fever, dysentery and the deadliest disease, cholera, raged.

Panama in 1852 was a town of contrasts. Many of the structures were one-story, thatched roof, tumbledown adobes enclosed by low stone walls, but there were also great stone buildings, paved streets, and a lively, established society. "Gambling appears to be the principle business done by the natives," observed one goldseeker as he passed through.[49] The American newspaper of the day reported that the summer of 1852 was an especially active one in Panama City with an estimated 10,000 natives, 350 permanent resident "foreigners" (mostly Americans), hundreds of California-bound passengers milling around, and building going on at a rapid pace. All kinds of

44. *PUSG*, I, 288.
45. *Ibid.*, 252.
46. Lewis, *Sheffield*, 9-10.
47. Howarth, *Panama*, 182.
48. *PUSG*, I, 252.
49. Sturdivant, *Journal*, 8.

transportation agents, general agents, and commission merchants were scrambling for business and trying to handle the rush demands. At least 137 foreign traders, mostly Americans, were listed on the tax rolls. The center of business, and indeed the center of town, was the Plaza dominated by the ancient cathedral with its twin bell towers. Merchandise of every description was being handled under the tropic sun and between rain showers as it was off-loaded from ships: cases of soap, sacks of rice, barrels of sugar, kegs of fresh butter, tea, pickles, dried apples, saddles, ropes, boots, shoes, pens, pencils, and ink. Popular items for sale included Havana cigars, a favorite of Grant's, "best London made clothing," and hardware items of all kinds. Ice from Boston or Sitka was being sold by the glass or by the pound, "two dimes a drink," and gin, sherry, port and other wines were in ample supply. On July 28, Grant had no trouble buying 249 blankets to replace those lost or damaged by the rains.[50]

The streets were dirty, the natives (mestizos) were mostly disagreeable, and the few Spanish seemed not too interested in the crowds of Americans. There was a goodly supply of cheap, fresh, and delicious fruit. Restaurants advertised the most careful preparation and full variety menus: the most popular were the Louisiana, the Aspinwall, and the New World. Hotels touted their natural air conditioning. Booth's Western on Main Street boasted it was "airy and cool and the bar is supplied with the best Liquors that are imported." Smith's Franklin House, on the Plaza, was in "the most healthy part of the city of Panama [with] the most airy and pleasant [rooms] . . . the breeze passing through it from every quarter."

Not surprisingly, the most important business of the City was that of moving people and freight. Taber & Perkins specialized in "baggage and merchandise forwarded between Gorgona and Panama with the greatest dispatch . . . saddle mules at command . . . children carried across the Isthmus in safety." Also, Herman C. Evers, manager of the semi-weekly express between Panama and Aspinwall, promoted his "number of fine boats . . . on the Chagres River . . . the boats connect at Gorgona with mule trains . . . an ample number . . . always ready for immediate use." Pacific Mail advertised their improved facilities at Taboga "capable of sustaining with perfect safety, the largest vessel in the Pacific Ocean." Even the infant Panama Railroad advertised their new "train of passenger cars."

The English-language newspaper, *Panama Star*, was published about once a week and chronicled the civic issues of the day: unfair and excessive taxes on foreigners; the new Panama Water Stock Company, "the second most important venture on the Isthmus," behind the railroad, of course; and the dismal record of the New Granada government on public works improvements,

50. *PUSG*, I, 251.

including the infamous "mud hole," a particularly troublesome spot Grant's party squashed through on the Cruces road.[51]

Meanwhile, Bonneville's party had reached Panama City on July 20 and was barged to the *Golden Gate* which was standing off Taboga to transport the troops to San Francisco. But now disaster struck these troops resting from their wet march: on their second day aboard, cholera broke out. Dr. Tripler had not arrived, so civilian medical help was enlisted.

Captain Wallen, sent ahead by the quartermaster, later recalled that as he neared Panama word reached him that the epidemic had broken out there also. His company moved directly to the ship and "that night one of my men was taken with the cholera, and by daylight the next morning there were several cases on board."[52] Delia Sheffield described the scene in Panama Bay:

Captain Grant, as quartermaster, and the surgeons did everything in their power to check the spread of the disease, and to alleviate the sufferings of the stricken ones. Too much praise cannot be given them for their tireless energy and great presence of mind during this outbreak of cholera. It was not an easy task to control almost seven hundred men during a siege of cholera, for they grew nervous and panic-stricken and Captain Grant had not only the sick ones to contend with but also the well.[53]

The drum-major's wife, Mrs. Elderkin, related that "Captain Grant had a tremendous responsibility . . . but he did the work with as much system as though he had been quartered at" an established army post. She saw the quartermaster as a man of iron, seldom sleeping, who seemed to take a personal interest in each case. "He was like a ministering angel to us all."[54]

Captain Wallen told of an incident that touched Ulysses most personally:

Grant was one of the coolest men in all these trying emergencies I ever saw. I remember during that dismal time in Panama bay that he, a Major Gore and myself sat playing a friendly game of euchre, when Major Gore suddenly dropped his hand, turned pale and said: "My God, I have got the Cholera!" Grant, in the most nonchalant way, undertook to quiet his fears by saying: "No, Major, you have only eaten something that does not agree with you." But the doctor was summoned, and although everything possible was done, Gore died before morning, the only officer we lost.[55]

The *Panama Herald*, in a July 27, 1852, editorial, reported that the 4th Infantry had been pouring into Panama City and moving out to the *Golden Gate* all week:

A portion of these troops came through in good time, and apparently in the

51. The description of Panama City in the summer of 1852, *Panama Star*, June 17, 26, 1852, the Honnald Library, Claremont, Calif.
52. Burr, *Grant*, 113–14.
53. Lewis, *Sheffield*, 10.
54. Garland, "Grant's Quiet Years," 408.
55. Burr, *Grant*, 114.

enjoyment of health. A goodly number, however, sickened and died on the road . . . [The number of dead] must have been considerable . . . There is great fault somewhere, and just censure should be meted out . . . The whole business reflects great discredit upon the United States . . ."[56]

Edward Flint, the steamship company agent, became concerned about the contamination of the *Golden Gate* and insisted on moving everybody to a hulk (the company called it a storeship) off Taboga in Panama Bay while the ship was fumigated. Later, that makeshift hospital became so crowded with sick that the troops and their families were moved to tents on smaller Flamenco Island.[57] Flamenco was the outer one of a group of small, rocky islands a few miles offshore from the city. Flamenco was utilized by the Pacific Mail as a major base beginning in early 1853 when the company moved from Taboga, the larger island farther out in the bay. Eventually the new base had storehouses, carpenter and blacksmith shops, overhaul facilities, and a large inventory of coal, but in 1852 Flamenco was barren, with only a few houses and some farmland.

Since a wide band of mud flats surrounded Panama City and the tide constantly deposited more silt, it was difficult for ships to lie in close and for passengers and baggage to be boarded. Small steamers transported cargo to the ships anchored in the bay. Flamenco Island played an important part in this arrangement as long as Pacific Mail operated a Panama run.

By August 3, the disease seemed to run its course, but the experienced Pacific Mail agent, fearing its reappearance, would dispatch the *Golden Gate* with only 450 passengers (the number of berths available). The rest of the 4th's group was left behind with one company to act as attendants, the Pacific Mail agreeing to supply these people with necessities of life and to bring them to California as quickly as possible.

The wooden "steam clipper" *Golden Gate,* with her spread-eagle figurehead, was a new and popular ship held in high regard by knowledgeable travelers and looked like an uncrowded paradise to the 4th. New York-built in 1850–51 at a cost of $483,000, she was the first sidewheel steamer designed for the Panama-California route after the true nature of the trade was known. Sleeker and longer than the *Ohio, Golden Gate,* at 2,067 tons and 269 feet long, was considered large, swift, comfortable.[58]

After spending three weeks on the Isthmus, on August 5, Bonneville's

56. *Ulysses S. Grant Association Newsletter,* Carbondale, Ill., (Jan., 1969), 1–2 (hereafter cited as *Newsletter*).
57. In *Memoirs,* I, 198, Grant incorrectly called this island "Flamingo"; several maps of the day did also. The correct name was, and is, Flamenco. See Dr. Kemble, National Geographic, and Anderson's *Old Panama* maps, among others.
58. Information on the *Golden Gate* from the following sources: Kemble, *Panama Route,* 228; Lewis, *Sea Routes,* 260; and Robert W. Parkinson in *Gold Rush Steamers* (San Francisco, 1958); David I. Folkman, Jr., *The Nicaragua Route* (Salt Lake City, 1972), 34.

regiment, having lost almost one hundred soldiers to cholera, departed for California. About 35,000 travelers made an Isthmus crossing that year but none suffered more than the 4th Infantry. The crossing was over, but a lifelong impression had been made upon the young captain as "he for the first time came into his own as a commander of men."[59] Hodges recalled that: "General Grant in his late years talked more about his experiences on the Isthmus than any of his great campaigns during the War of the Rebellion."[60] One biographer of Grant said the crossing "left him with the permanent dream of a canal in which travellers wouldn't have to set foot on those jungle shores."[61]

News of the 4th Infantry's problems on the Isthmus was quick to reach San Francisco. On August 14, the *Daily Alta California* headlined its report that the *Golden Gate* was detained in Panama. The newspaper's great concern was with slow mails and not with casualties; they reported the delay was "on account of the lamentable mismanagement . . . on the part of the Agent, who had charge of the United States Mails."

Pacific Mail's *Columbia* was the bearer of the news. Mr. Burns, her purser, reported that the *Golden Gate* was "detained in consequence of the baggage belonging to the troops not having arrived." The *Columbia*'s Captain Dall gave a fuller report when he stepped ashore at San Francisco. The captain told of the *Ohio*'s arrival at Aspinwall and how all troops were given sufficient rations to make their way across the Isthmus. "Before arriving at their destinations, the provisions of many failed, when they indulged themselves in eating heartily of all kinds of fruit. The consequence was that many were affected with a species of the cholera . . . The *Golden Gate* will be detained at Panama until she can obtain a clean bill of health and until the baggage of the troops can be placed on board." The steamship company was not blamed for the delay. The newspaper editorialized: "There is great credit

---

59. Lloyd Lewis, *Letters from Lloyd Lewis* (Boston, 1950), 78.
60. Hodges as cited in note 8.
61. Lloyd Lewis, *Letters*, 77–78. In his first presidential message to Congress, Grant recommended an American canal connecting the two oceans. David McCullough, *The Path Between the Seas* (New York, 1977), 26–27, reports that "Grant . . . was indeed the first President to address himself seriously to the [canal] subject . . . [H]e wanted it in the proper place . . . and he wanted it under American control. 'To Europeans the benefits . . . of the proposed canal are great,' he was to write, 'to Americans they are incalculable.'" Grant sent seven canal expeditions to Central America between 1870 and 1875. And, his connection to the Isthmus did not cease when he left the White House. In John Y. Simon, ed., *The Personal Memoirs of Julia Dent Grant* (New York, 1975), 322, Julia recalls that in 1880 Grant "was offered the presidency of the Panama Canal Company in the United States . . ." McCullough records (p. 127) that the former president "flatly declined the offer, a decision Grant explained . . . 'while I would like to have my name associated with the successful completion of a ship canal between the two oceans, I was not willing to connect it with a failure and one I believe subscribers would lose all they put in.'" Grant turned down the $25,000 salary offer out-of-hand; his annual income at the time was $6,000. But he was right. The Comité Américain, part of Ferdinand de Lesseps's ill-fated effort, was a costly failure.

due the Pacific Mail Company for their prompt exertions in relieving and taking care of the sick and suffering."[62] Bonneville's official report supported this conclusion. Almost as an afterthought the names of the Sisters of Charity who died on the Isthmus were published. And, Mr. and Mrs. Lynch left three orphans.

Five days later, August 19, the *Daily Alta California* headlined: "Arrival of the *Golden Gate*; Quick Passage from Panama; Arrival of the 4th Regiment U. S. Infantry;" and, in a feature article entitled "The Troubles of the *Golden Gate*," told San Francisco the story. Captain C. P. Patterson of the *Golden Gate* reported he was ready for the return trip to California on July 17, but it was the twentieth before 650 of the 4th Infantry arrived. "The remainder of the regiment, some 100 in number, with the sick and camp attendants were received in course of the ensuing week, great delay having occurred in their march over the Isthmus. On the 20th one of the soldiers died of cholera . . . three more dying the succeeding night." Patterson then repeated the story of the move to the hospital vessel and the apparent checking of the disease, but after July 27, "a change of weather unfortunately caused the cholera to reappear with increased severity, where, with the concurrence of Col. Bonneville, all of the troops were landed upon Flamenco Island. Twenty-nine more soldiers died there along with two crew members while the *Golden Gate*, was thoroughly fumigated for several days in succession." Captain Patterson concluded that the deaths were "solely attributed to the exposure and imprudence of the troops while marching over the Isthmus." The newspaper reported that: "The company certainly did all in their power . . . and deserve great credit for their prompt and efficient exertions. It is a cause of congratulations for all that the results . . . were not extended with more disastrous effects." The casualties were noted: "Eighty-four of the troops died . . . [and] Lieut. Gore . . . died on board the *Golden Gate*." The story closed with the news that "the invalids were left at the island of Flamenco in the Bay of Panama, in charge of Lieuts. Boneycastle, Huger and Surgeon Tripler."[63]

On August 26, Bonneville submitted his official report on the troop movement from New York to California. He reported the July 5 departure of 651 men, their arrival at Aspinwall, and filled in the details of the disaster with the baggage and cholera. Bonneville continued his report telling of the reluctance of the Pacific Mail to dispatch the ship with more men than could be accommodated in bunks available and of the arrangements made to care for those who would remain behind. "The Agents having agreed to furnish the troops left behind with everything necessary for their comfort and to transport them to [Benicia, California] as soon as possible, I approved the

62. *San Francisco Daily Alta California*, Aug. 14, 1852.
63. *Ibid.*, Aug. 19, 1852.

plan." The 4th's commander summarized his casualties and stated that "the Agents of the Pacific Mail Steam Ship Company made extraordinary exertions to make the troops comfortable, and subjected themselves to considerable expense in their efforts to administer to the wants of our sick."[64] Not a word for the quartermaster he left on the river to deal with the disaster.

Bonneville's officers did not agree. Hodges called the Pacific Mail management "dilatory and incompetent," and the regimental officers formally charged the steamship company with contract failure.

Almost two weeks after the 4th had sailed and was unable to defend itself, the *Panama Herald* thought it had found out who was to blame for the fiasco. On August 17, it published a scathing attack on the officers of the regiment and particularly the quartermaster, charging that the troops were:

Deserted, . . . by every commissioned officer, . . . [while] The officers and their wives came over in the usual time, on mules, in good health and condition. Even the regimental quartermaster, Capt. GRANT, could not tarry to attend to his duty, but must come through and await the arrival of the troops on this side! . . . With *Quartermaster* GRANT, we have not done: Unfitted by either natural ability or education for the post he occupied, he evinced his incapacity at every movement. Totally inefficient himself he left his business to his Sergeant, and then repudiated the expense he had incurred at a Hotel for necessary comfort and attention to sick men, women and children, though promising to settle the account before he left, yet in the end sneaking off on board without even calling at the Hotel to see the bill, and when caught on board the steamer, refusing to pay but a moiety of the expenses ordered by his official![65]

Grant later wrote to Julia that she probably had seen published reports reflecting upon the 4th Infantry officers while crossing the Isthmus and alleging that, "even Capt. Grant ran off, and left the men to take care of themselves." He told his wife the story was untrue and that the papers would soon carry the facts.[66]

The indignant 4th Infantry officers' formal resolution of denial appeared in the *San Francisco Herald* on November 1, 1852, and it called the *Panama Herald*'s story "a scandalous and malicious falsehood." The resolutions pointed out that all of the regiment's officers, with three exceptions, stayed with the troops "and shared with them the fatigues of the march." The exceptions were one sick officer, the escort for the officers' families, and Captain Grant, "who was detained at Cruces to take charge of the baggage." Further, the officers pointed out that Captain Grant "was the last officer who left Cruces, he having been obliged to stay there five days in the discharge of his official duties" because of the Pacific Mail's failure to provide for the

64. Lt. Col. B. L. E. Bonneville to Capt. Edward D. Townsend, Aug. 26, 1852, Pacific Division, Letters Received, Record Group 393, National Archives, Washington, D.C.
65. *Newsletter*, (Jan., 1969), 13–14.
66. *PUSG*, I, 270–71.

regimental baggage. "[A]nd while the troops left with the baggage were waiting at Cruces, a number of them died of cholera."[67]

This was Grant's first newspaper controversy and although he was "undoubtedly pleased that his fellow officers defended him, Grant did not publish a word in his own behalf, a pattern he invariably followed in later controversies."[68]

The *Panama Herald* understandably wanted to "place the blame for the disastrous loss of life on the Isthmus on something other than the unhealthy climate or local business interests; the paper could lose heavily if the experience of the 4th Infantry influenced future travelers to use other routes to the Pacific Coast."[69]

The charges against Grant were ironic, however, because he ". . . probably displayed more personal bravery and calm thinking in the fever-ridden backwater of Cruces than was called for on the major battlefields of the Civil War."[70] And, he "was never in greater personal danger while serving in the army than during his passage across the Isthmus of Panama in 1852."[71]

67. *Newsletter*, (Jan., 1969), 15.
68. *Ibid.*, 16.
69. *Ibid.*
70. *Ibid.*
71. *Ibid.*, (Oct., 1967), 1.

IV

General Ulysses S. Grant Diplomat Extraordinaire

By Horatio E. Wirtz

One hundred years ago in the summer of 1879, General and Mrs. Ulysses S. Grant were in the final stage of their two-year pleasure trip around the world which was to end unexpectedly in a burst of high diplomacy by General Grant. When they embarked on this trip in May of 1877, General Grant naturally thought he would be greeted abroad as a private citizen, and just as naturally he was not. As general in chief of the Armies of the United States and then president for two terms he had been in the public eye for sixteen years. Undoubtedly he was the most famous living American, and, in fact, a world celebrity. By the time they reached China in April, 1879, the Grants had been entertained by more than seventeen emperors and kings, plus countless princes, dukes, archdukes, grand dukes, sultans, maharajahs, prime ministers, and presidents.[1] All this attention and adulation heaped on him General Grant neatly turned aside by always saying publicly that the honors were for America and his countrymen, not himself.

In China a new challenge awaited him. After being welcomed by 100,000 Chinese in Shanghai, General Grant proceeded to Tientsin where he was immediately entertained by Viceroy Li Hung Chang. Unknown to the general, on the very day the Grants were sailing to Tientsin, the Japanese were forcibly removing King Sho Tai of the Ryukyu Islands (Loochoo Islands) to Japan as part of their campaign to assert complete sovereignty over those islands long claimed by China.

The Chinese had followed closely General Grant's progress across India,

---

1. John Russell Young, *Around the World with General Grant* (New York, 1879), II, *passim*.

and on to Burma, Siam, Singapore, and Saigon. They had decided to enlist his aid against Japan in their confrontation over the status of the Ryukyus. Through his great prestige and authority they planned to "associate Grant and the United States with China's claims, by inference, if not by technical fact."[2] The Japanese, meanwhile, had apprised themselves of the Chinese designs and were preparing to take countermeasures when General Grant arrived in Japan. Of these secret Oriental intentions and stratagems General Grant knew nothing.

The Ryukyus are a chain of islands 650 miles long, extending southward from Kyushu in Japan to Taiwan. They divide the China Sea on the east from the Philippine Sea on the west. Their history is that of an independent island people whose geography unfortunately placed them between two far greater nations then emerging into a late nineteenth century power struggle. Into this delicate and dangerous situation came General Grant.

No sooner had the Grants arrived in Tientsin aboard the U.S. warship *Ashuelot* than the viceroy came to call. Li Hung Chang, often called "the Bismarck of the East," was one of the two most important men in China, the other being Prince Kung, regent and ruler of the land. The viceroy was a famous general who had put down the Taiping Rebellion in the 1860s and, hence, felt an affinity for General Grant. During their many conversations he informed the general of the current crisis between China and Japan and asked for his help. General Grant said that anything he could do in the interest of peace would be a pleasure. However, he carefully noted that he was no longer an officer of state, but merely a private citizen.[3] Li Hung Chang was, nevertheless, sufficiently impressed with the former president's willingness to help that he informed Prince Kung in Peking of the demarche he had made and the general's response.

Prince Kung awaited the arrival of the Grants in Peking with expectation. At his second meeting with General Grant he raised the Ryukyu question. From then on between ceremonial dinners and sightseeing, the prince and general conferred about the crucial problem. The principal Chinese demands were that the deposed king be returned, that the Japanese withdraw their troops and declaration of exclusive sovereignty, and that the traditional investiture ceremonies be restored. General Grant was largely and wisely noncommittal but thought that "any course short of national humiliation or national destruction was better than war," and "war especially between two nations like China and Japan would be a measureless misfortune."[4] Finally, after reminding Prince Kung that he was only a traveler, he said he would inform himself on the subject and converse with the Japanese. "I have no

2. George H. Kerr, *Okinawa, The History of an Island People* (Rutland, Vt. and Tokyo, 1958), 387.
3. Young, II, 411.
4. *Ibid.*

idea," he continued, "what their argument is. They, of course, have an argument. I do not suppose that the rulers are inspired by a desire wantonly to injure China. I will acquaint myself with the Chinese side of the case, as your Imperial Highness and the Viceroy have presented it, and promise to present it. I will do what I can to learn the Japanese side. Then, if I can in conversation with the Japanese authorities do anything that will be a service to the cause of peace, you may depend upon my good offices. But, as I have said, I have no knowledge on the subject, and no idea what opinion I may entertain when I have studied it."[5] The general then called attention to the settlement of the Alabama Claims of the United States against England which were settled by arbitration. "That arbitration . . . between nations may not satisfy either party at the time," he said, "but it satisfies the conscience of the world, and must commend itself, as we grow in civilization, more and more, as the means of adjusting international disputes."[6]

After they returned to Tientsin, the Grants were again entertained by the viceroy, and Mrs. Grant and other American ladies were given a dinner party by Madame Li Hung Chang, an unprecedented honor. Finally, the Grants prepared to leave on the U.S. warship *Richmond* for Japan, and Li Hung Chang sailed out in his yacht surrounded by gunboats to say good-bye. After a prodigious firing of salutes, he went on board the *Richmond*. Following an inspection of the ship during which he showed great interest in how the guns worked, he again brought up the Ryukyu dispute. General Grant expressed his thanks for the great honors he had received in China and assured the viceroy he would not forget what had been said by him and Prince Kung.

The Chinese had been greatly impressed with General Grant. They were accustomed to the superior, arrogant, contumacious attitude of the European powers and their representatives. All the great powers had extracted extra-territorial rights from them, insisted they allow the importation of opium, insisted they allow missionaries to propagate the worship of Jesus Christ when they already had Confucius and Buddha, and humiliated them with indemnities, threats, and superior gun power. No European or American public figure of the prestige of General Grant had ever deigned to visit them before. They knew he was a great general and powerful soldier and would not have been surprised if he had arrived in the full panoply of the High Victorian general—a uniform blazing with decorations, gold braid, sashes, feathers, and sword at his side. Rather they saw a quiet and sympathetic gentleman in evening clothes smoking his cigar.

On 21 June 1879 General Grant and his party arrived in Nagasaki where the Japanese had prepared a "royal" welcome. Throughout his long tour there had been puzzlement over what honors he should be accorded. A former

---

5. *Ibid.*, 412.
6. *Ibid.*

president of the United States has no title, no rank, no authority; he is, indeed, only a private citizen. Nevertheless, throughout his trip he had been given twenty-one gun salutes and met by honor guards and military bands playing national anthems. The Japanese had solved their problem by deciding to treat him as a "guest of the nation" and Prince of the Blood. At Nagasaki the guns saluted, the yardarms of the ships were manned, and a scarlet carpeting laid. On the second day dinner was given by the governor of Nagasaki. In attendance were Prince Dati, representing the emperor, the Japanese ambassador to the United States who had been called home to be present during the visit, Judge John Armor Bingham, the American ambassador appointed to his post by President Grant in 1873, and the highest dignitaries of Nagasaki. After a speech by the governor, General Grant made his first speech in Japan. In it he expressed the "spirit of sympathy, support, and conciliation" with which America regarded Japan. As her nearest neighbor in the West, he said, "America has much to gain in the East—no nation has greater interests; but America has nothing to gain except what comes from the cheerful acquiescence of the Eastern people and insures them as much benefit as it does us." Continuing he asserted, "No nation needs from the outside powers justice and kindness more than Japan, because the work that has made such marvelous progress in the past few years is a work in which we are deeply concerned, in the success of which we see a new era in civilization and which we should encourage."[7] The speech was well received. The *Tokyo Times* said it was "one of the most important and significant statements of conviction respecting the rights of Japan."[8] At the outset of his visit with its attendant diplomatic mission, General Grant had struck the right note.

In Tokyo more sumptuous preparations had been completed. Because they did not want the Grants to have to stay in Japanese-style accommodations, the Japanese had converted a former naval academy situated on an island in the middle of a lake into a Europeanized palace, Enryokan. In a land noted for its tea ceremony they had manufactured a Western-style silver tea service engraved with the imperial chrysanthemum for the use of Mrs. Grant. On the Fourth of July, a date chosen for its American significance, the general and Mrs. Grant were received by the emperor and empress. The emperor advanced and shook hands with the general, a small thing but unheard of in Japan. Three days later the emperor and General Grant presided over a grand review of the new Japanese army. In Europe the general had declined on numerous occasions to review troops and somewhat discomfited his hosts there. Here he sensed that would not do. During the breakfast following the review, the emperor told

7. *Ibid.*, 481.
8. Richard T. Chang, "General Grant's 1879 Visit to Japan," *Monumenta Nipponica*, XXIV, 4 (1969), 377.

him he wished to have private conferences with him, to which of course, General Grant freely assented.

At this time the Emperor Meiji was a young man twenty-seven years old. During his eleven years as emperor, feudalism had been abolished, a strong program of Westernization begun, and power concentrated in the emperor's hands. For reasons best known to himself he took a great liking to General Grant, exactly thirty years his senior; hence, an exceptional role in the future of Japan devolved on the former president.

Visiting schools, factories, shrines, monuments, and gardens, General Grant familiarized himself with what was going on in Japan. In discussions with the emperor and his advisers he gave forthright advice and observations on what is now designated as a wide-ranging series of subjects. The Japanese at this time were beginning the formulation of their constitution, later known as the Meiji Constitution. General Grant discovered that the question of creating an assembly with legislative powers aroused intense feelings among the Japanese. He told the emperor that this must be carefully considered. Once given, he noted, rights of suffrage and representation could not be withdrawn. As a first step he recommended calling an elective assembly which would meet with the emperor's ministers to discuss the question. Suffrage might be given gradually hand-in-hand with education.[9]

Another crucial problem was the extraterritorial rights forced on Japan by the Western powers. The United States had shown itself willing to revise these. The general told the emperor that in crossing India and Southeast Asia he had seen the growth of European influence and dominance. Some things were to admire, and some to regret. "But," he said, "since I left India I have seen things that made my blood boil, in the way the European powers attempt to degrade the Asiatic nations. I would not believe such a policy possible. It seems to have no other aim than the extinction of the independence of the Asiatic nations. . . . It seems incredible that rights which at home we regard as essential to our independence and to our national existence, which no European nation, no matter how small, would surrender, are denied to China and Japan."[10]

One of the great injustices inflicted by the extraterritorial treaties was the limit placed on control of commerce and tariffs. The treaties limited to 5 percent the tariff Japan could place on imports. Said General Grant to the emperor, "A nation's life may often depend upon her commerce, and she is entitled to all the profit that can come out of it. Japan especially seems to me in a position where the control of her commerce would enable her statesmen to relieve the people of one great burden—the land-tax. The effect of so great a tax is to impoverish the people and limit agriculture. When the farmer must

9. Young, II, 543.
10. *Ibid.*, 543–44.

give a half of his crop for taxes he is not apt to raise more than will keep him alive. If the land-tax could be lessened, I have no doubt that agriculture would increase in Japan, and the increase would make the people richer, make them buy and consume more, and thus in the end benefit commerce as well. It seems to me that if the commerce of Japan were made to yield its proportion of the revenue, as the commerce of England and France and the United States, this tax could be lessened."[11] General Grant could not have been more right. At this time only 3.8 percent of Japan's revenue came from custom duties while 64.8 percent came from the land tax. On the other hand the United States received 55 percent of its revenues from tariffs.[12]

General Grant advised the Japanese to state their case publicly before the world, and if necessary, announce that the treaties were at an end. The Japanese were fearful that this would bring foreign fleets, that the English would bombard Tokyo as they had Shimonoseki. "If there is one thing more certain than another," reasoned the general, "it is that England is in no humor to make war upon Japan for a tariff. I do not believe that under any circumstances Lord Beaconsfield would consent to such an enterprise. He has had two wars, neither of which have commended themselves to the English people. An Englishman does not value the glory that comes from Afghan and Zulu campaigns. To add to these a demonstration against Japan, because she had resolved to submit no longer to a condition bordering on slavery, would arouse against Lord Beaconsfield a feeling at home that would cost him his government. Just now, . . . is the best time. Lord Beaconsfield must soon go to the people. His Parliament is coming to an end, and even if he had adventurous spirits in his cabinet or in the diplomatic service disposed to push Japan, he would be compelled to control them. . . . Japan has peculiar claims upon the sympathy and respect of mankind, and if she would assert her sovereign rights she would find that her cause met the approval of mankind."[13] No wonder Sir Harry Parkes, the imperialistic and jingoistic British ambassador to Japan, wrote, "General Grant is here and is turning Japanese heads."[14]

From money and the tariffs the discussion naturally turned to the question of national indebtedness. General Grant's opinion was that Japan should at all cost avoid borrowing abroad. Foreign loans brought danger and humiliation. He cited Egypt where he had been entertained by the khedive and traveled extensively. The khedive had been allowed, even encouraged, to incur huge debts. The result was that Egypt was under the control of her creditor nations: England and France.

11. *Ibid.*, 544.
12. Chang, 384.
13. Young, II, 583.
14. Payson J. Treat, *Diplomatic Relations Between the United States and Japan, 1853–1895* (1932; reprint ed., Gloucester, Mass., 1963), II, 91.

Then came the Ryukyu problem with its threat of war and disaster. Reporting to the emperor that he had read and listened to the arguments of both sides, General Grant said that he did not think it correct for him to express an opinion on the substance of the matter. However, he felt strongly that China and Japan should avoid war and remain friends. To do this some sacrifices might be necessary. There were "powerful influences" at work which would not be sorry to see a war between China and Japan. A war would give them an excuse to intervene and more concessions would be extracted. "European powers have no interests in Asia, so far as I can judge, . . . that do not involve the humiliation of the Asiatic people," he said.[15] He did make one concrete suggestion: that a boundary running between the islands so as to give the Chinese a wide channel to the Pacific might be accepted by them. His final advice in conference was that China and Japan should come together without foreign intervention or participation and talk until they reached friendly settlement.

In addition to General Grant's conferences with the emperor and his advisers, the Grants were busy seeing the sights and being seen by the Japanese people. Their very natural comportment ingratiated them more and more with the Japanese. At the shrine of Nikko-Shimbashi General Grant was invited to cross the Divine Bridge leading to the Nikko Mausoleum, a privilege of Princes of the Blood, which he theoretically was. However, he graciously refused, saying he understood that only princes were allowed to cross. Such effacing behavior by a high-ranking Westerner startled the Japanese.[16] Among the many entertainments offered the Grants was a special performance at the Shintomiza Theater, the only Western-style theater in Japan. Scenes from General Grant's life were dramatized as having occurred in the life of an eleventh century Japanese warrior hero. At the close of the evening General Grant presented the theater with what Julia Grant described as a "handsome red cloth drop curtain."[17] Another festivity was a public reception, the first such event ever held in Japan. A Tokyo Citizens Committee had invited fifteen hundred people for the night of 8 July 1879. After eight years of strenuous White House entertaining, the Grants were quite at home in such a situation. Although he spoke no Japanese, General Grant circulated freely shaking hands with everyone regardless of rank. This democratic procedure together with his simplicity and dignity created a tremendous impression. Julia Grant also contributed. Madame Shibusawa Eiichi, wife of the president of the Tokyo Chamber of Commerce, considered her "exceedingly graceful"[18]—for an American woman. Although not a trained diplomat, General Grant obviously conducted diplomacy on two levels: forthright

15. Chang, 381.
16. *Ibid.*, 379.
17. John Y. Simon, ed., *Personal Memoirs of Julia Dent Grant* (New York, 1975), 300.
18. Chang, 387.

advice in conferences, and innate tact and politeness in everyday behavior.

While the Grants were charming the Japanese, the Chinese made a move. In a formal letter they requested the United States to exercise its good offices in the Ryukyu dispute. American Secretary of State William M. Evarts accepted on the condition that Japan would also request American mediation. Japan naturally did not make such a request because that would be an official recognition that there was a question of sovereignty involving the Ryukyus. To discuss the problem with General Grant, a friendly individual, was one thing; to ask officially for the United States to mediate was quite another.

Having studied the controversy and the arguments of both sides, General Grant composed a carefully worded identical letter, written in his lucid, concise style, addressed to the regent of China and the foreign minister of Japan. Dated 13 August 1879 the letter summed up his views and proposed a course of action China and Japan might follow. He advised the Chinese to withdraw certain offensive correspondence they had addressed to the Japanese the previous year. He suggested that the two countries appoint commissioners who should meet and discuss the problem. As he had said in conversation already, he strongly warned against allowing any foreigners or foreign countries to become parties to the dispute itself. He mentioned Japan's friendliness toward China, and suggested that China emulate Japan in a program of modernization and resistance to foreign controls.[19]

The grand finale of General Grant's historic visit was a huge celebration in Ueno Park on 25 August 1879. This all-day festivity was paid for by popular subscription. The English order of the day was somewhat incongruously headed: "PROGRAMME OF THE FÊTE CHAMPÉTRE AT UYENO PARK."[20] General Grant and his party drove from his palace in imperial state carriages preceded and surrounded by an escort of cavalry. At the park a committee awaited, and invited General and Mrs. Grant to plant two memorial trees. The general planted a Lawson cypress, and Julia an evergreen magnolia. When the emperor arrived, the army and navy bands played alternately. After the emperor received Japanese over the age of eighty, he took his seat in an amphitheater with General Grant on his right. Various sports and "feats of horsemanship" were performed. The day ended with a supper and brilliant fireworks.

On 30 August 1879 the Grants made a formal farewell call on the emperor and empress. For this occasion the general had written his speech in advance. Since he declared he had no "verbal memory," his usual practice was to speak impromptu; in fact, when advance copies of speeches to be made to him were furnished, he usually refused to read them, thinking that would take away from the spontaneity of his reply. Realizing, however, the importance of this

19. Series 1B, Ulysses S. Grant Papers, Library of Congress.
20. *Ibid.*

occasion, he had prepared. In his remarks to the emperor he, of course, offered thanks for the great hospitality shown him, and then commented on Japan's possibilities for the future, her assets in "fertile soil, . . . undeveloped mineral resources, numerous and fine harbors, . . . sea-coast abounding in fish of an almost endless variety, and, above all, an industrious, ingenious, contented, and frugal population." He then sounded the theme uppermost in Japanese minds. "With all these nothing is wanted to insure great progress except wise direction by the government, peace at home and abroad, and non-interference in the internal and domestic affairs of the country by the outside nations."[21] Nothing could have pleased the Japanese more than that sentiment. Four days later General and Mrs. Grant sailed aboard the steamer *City of Tokio* for San Francisco where thousands of red-blooded Americans were on hand to greet them, and Julia Grant wrote, "We entered the Golden Gate to the roar of artillery, the smoke of which entirely obscured everything."[22]

To his identical letters suggesting how the Ryukyu problem might be resolved both the Chinese and Japanese responded. Li Hung Chang wrote offering thanks and saying, "Your Excellency's remark that both countries should make mutual concessions in the interests of peace, is most wise and just." And he continued, "My Government is unanimously in favor of undertaking such measures as will establish China as a great Power, and thus will realize the kind wishes to that effect expressed by your Excellency. . . ."[23] He ended, hoping General Grant might succeed to the next presidency. Prince Kung wrote in the same vein saying, ". . . it is right that the advice in your letter should be followed and that China and Japan should deliberate upon some plan whereby relations of perpetual friendship may be preserved between the two countries."[24] The Japanese foreign minister, Yoshida Kiyonara, wrote analyzing the most recent communication from China as a result of General Grant's mediation and noted happily, "On the whole it does not seem to me that the Chinese Govt. intends to insist upon any fixed proposition whatever of the adjustment of the question."[25] The following year Japan, adhering to General Grant's suggestions, opened negotiations with China in Peking. After two months of conferring, draft proposals were drawn up giving the southern islands of the Ryukyu to China, and Okinawa and the northern islands to Japan. Japan was also to receive "most favored nation" treatment in trade, a concession already enjoyed by European nations. This document was to be signed 31 October 1880, but after Byzantine maneuvers within the high councils of the Chinese imperial government, China repudiated its

21. Young, II, 603.
22. Julia Dent Grant, 307.
23. Li Hung Chang to Grant, Aug. 23, 1879, in possession of Mrs. Edith Grant Griffiths, Arlington, Va.
24. Prince Kung to Grant, Sept. 20, 1879, *ibid.*
25. Yoshida Kiyonara to Grant, Sept. 19, 1879, *ibid.*

representatives and did not sign. On 5 January 1881, the Japanese unilaterally declared the Ryukyu question closed. Nothing significant occurred in the Ryukyus until 1945 when 12,000 Americans were killed and 36,000 wounded wresting Okinawa from the Japanese.

The epilogue of General Grant's exercise in diplomacy and elder statesmanship stretched into the future. In 1880 the Japanese ministry recommended borrowing fifty million yen abroad. In an imperial rescript the Emperor Meiji vetoed it writing: "Last year Grant spoke of the harm of foreign debts. His words are still fresh in my ears."[26] In accord with General Grant's suggestion the emperor issued a decree promising a national assembly in 1890. During the thirty-eight days General Grant lay dying at Mount McGregor in the Adirondack Mountains of New York State, the emperor instructed the Japanese envoy in Washington to travel four times to see the general. In 1889 the new Japanese constitution was promulgated and in 1890 the first election was held. During the writing of the constitution the emperor was heard to say often, "On this question Grant said. . . . On that question Grant taught me. . . ."[27]

The war between China and Japan, averted in 1879, came in 1895 over Korea. As General Grant had foreseen, China was grievously hurt. Russia, France, and Germany did intervene; China lost territory and had to make more concessions. Japan did not get all she wanted.

The year following this disaster Li Hung Chang at the age of seventy-four made a visit to the United States where he was received as a "guest of the nation." While in New York City, he made at his request a visit to the grave of General Grant. Carried in his sedan chair from Riverside Drive to the entrance of the tomb, he then descended to the crypt laying a wreath on the casket. In a notable expression of his feeling he stood in silent meditation for twenty minutes beside the coffin. Having been accompanied by General Grant's son, Colonel Frederick D. Grant, he returned with him to his home on East Sixty-second Street to have tea with Julia Dent Grant.[28]

After ruling for forty-four years the Emperor Meiji, friend and admirer of General Grant, died in 1912. But the Japanese did not forget their American friend. The trees planted by the general and Julia grew strong and tall. On the fiftieth anniversary of the planting in 1929, the Japanese erected a memorial to General Grant by the trees lest future generations lose track of their significance. The memorial is of stone in the center of which is a bronze plaque with a bas-relief of the head and shoulders of General Grant. On either side are bronze tablets one in Japanese, the other in English which reads:

26. Chang, 385.
27. *Ibid.*
28. *Democrat and Chronicle*, Rochester, N.Y., Aug. 30, 1896.

MEMORIAL TREES PLANTED BY GENERAL AND MRS. ULYSSES S. GRANT

General Ulysses Simpson Grant, ex-President of the United States of America, arrived at Nagasaki in 1879, whereupon Meiji Tenno dispatched an Imperial envoy and a warship to greet him. On his arrival in Tokyo on July 3rd, the General was hailed with great enthusiasm by its leading citizens. Meiji Tenno welcomed him as the guest of the nation and placed the Hama Detached Palace at his disposal.

Imperial audiences, sight-seeing, and various kinds of entertainment were arranged for him. On August 25th, the final entertainment was held in honor of General and Mrs. Grant at Ueno Park, in which Meiji Tenno was graciously present.

In commemoration of this event, General Grant planted a hinoki (Cupressus Lawsoniana) and Mrs. Grant a gyokuran (Magnolia grandiflora), both of which have grown thick and tall. But few people now know the history of the trees. Therefore, we who had the privilege of participating in the welcome event fifty years ago, have erected this memorial tablet near them.

August 1929　　　　　　　　　　　　　　　　Viscount Eiichi Shibusawa
　　　　　　　　　　　　　　　　　　　　　　Baron Takashi Masuda[29]

In 1935 six years after the dedication of the monument occurred the fiftieth anniversary of General Grant's death. A memorial service was held and a pamphlet published which said in part: "As we look back . . . from the beginning of our history no one has ever spoken to the Emperor as personally and candidly on so many subjects as did the General. . . . The great service of the General as a benefactor of new Japan should be remembered forever."[30]

Both trees and monument survived the bombing of Tokyo during World War II. Since 1946 the Industry Club of Japan and the Shibusawa Ryumonsha have sponsored a service held at the monument on American Memorial Day, May 30. "Important" Americans are invited and a luncheon follows at the Industry Club of Japan.

The trees planted by General Grant and Julia are now over one hundred years old. They attest that General Grant was not only what Viscount Montgomery of Alamein called him, "a soldier's soldier, a general's general";[31] but also a diplomat and statesman of tact, perception, and great common sense.

29. From a photograph taken Feb., 1979, in possession of the author.
30. Chang, 390.
31. Viscount Montgomery of Alamein, *A History of Warfare* (Cleveland and New York, 1968), 438.

Trees planted by Ulysses S. and Julia Dent Grant in Ueno Park, Tokyo, during their visit to Japan in 1879.

Memorial erected in 1929 in Ueno Park to commemorate the fiftieth anniversary of Grant's visit.
Photographs in possession of Horatio E. Wirtz.

V

First Impressions of
Three Days' Fighting

Quartermaster General Meigs's
"Journal of the Battle of Chattanooga"

Edited by John M. Hoffmann

Introduction

On November 23-25, 1863, Major General Ulysses S. Grant's forces at Chattanooga successfully broke a siege by General Braxton Bragg's army, driving the bewildered foe into northern Georgia. On November 26, Quartermaster General Montgomery C. Meigs reported the Union triumph to Secretary of War Edwin M. Stanton. This dispatch, immediately released to the press, soon became the standard account of the climactic days of the Chattanooga campaign: the advance on Orchard Knob had been a "surprise in open daylight," the battle on Lookout Mountain was fought "above the clouds," and the assault on Missionary Ridge took place "as in an amphitheater."[1] Yet before Meigs pitched upon these vivid terms for a succession of truly spectacular events, he dashed off a parallel but fuller, more personal, and more revealing description of the fighting. This illuminating source for the study of the conflict, especially of Grant's generalship on the last day, is here published for the first time.[2]

1. U.S. War Department, *The War of the Rebellion: A Compilation of the Official Records of the Union and Confederate Armies* (Washington, 1880-1901), I, xxxi, part 2, 77-78 (hereafter cited as *O.R.* followed by series and vol.).
2. The journal and other manuscripts, except as otherwise noted, are in the Meigs Papers in the

I

The significance of Meigs's journal, and of his famous report, derives at least partly from his presence in Chattanooga before the battles and from his closeness to Grant and to Stanton. Late in August, 1863, Stanton sent Meigs to inspect the principal Union armies in the field and their supply depots. He reached the Army of the Cumberland in Chattanooga on September 25, just after the disastrous battle of Chickamauga. Instructed to improve operations of the quartermasters in his purview, he gave most attention to problems of supplying Major General William S. Rosecrans's troops, who were "closely beleaguered" by Bragg's army. Although it was "flushed with the confidence of victory," having been "permitted to gather the spoils of the battle-field," Meigs at first reported that Rosecrans's men were also "confident," and that Chattanooga was a "fortified base" close to the heart of the Confederacy. But soon he painted a gloomier picture: having lost control of the Tennessee River near Chattanooga, the Union army could only be supplied by a long "circuitous route" overland. "Forage grows scarce," he wrote on October 9. "Many horses are unserviceable and some have died. . . . If the artillery and ammunition horses give out the army cannot move."[3]

Before Stanton received or fully comprehended this predicament, he instructed Meigs to return to Washington, where "movements on the Potomac" had created a new "crisis." Accordingly, Meigs left Chattanooga for Louisville. On October 16, however, Stanton directed that he remain in Tennessee, since "all reports indicate the necessity of a controlling and regulating mind" there.[4] Stanton referred to the handling of supplies, but he, Major General Henry W. Halleck, and President Abraham Lincoln had come to the same conclusion about the command of the western armies as a whole. To strengthen Rosecrans's forces, the government had already detached from the Army of the Potomac two corps under Major General Joseph Hooker, and Grant had responded to its call by sending from the Army of the Tennessee four divisions under Major General William T. Sherman. Grant had also been ordered from Vicksburg, and now Stanton rushed to Louisville to confer with him directly, meeting Meigs there as well. On October 18, before Grant and Meigs left for Chattanooga, Grant assumed command of the Military Division of the Mississippi, encompassing most of the armies in the west, and

Manuscript Division of the Library of Congress. The journal was copied for the Ulysses S. Grant Association with the assistance of Richard N. Sheldon of the National Historical Publications and Records Commission, while additional microfilming was arranged for the editor by Paul T. Heffron and O. H. Orr of the Manuscript Division. Russell F. Weigley of Temple University lent his support to the project, providing in particular the text of Meigs's diary entry for July 24, 1865, and the explanation regarding the date on the journal.
3. *O.R.*, I, xxix, part 2, 154-55; *ibid.*, I, xxix, part 1, 156; *ibid.*, III, iv, 879; *ibid.*, I, xxx, part 3, 890; *ibid.*, I, xxx, part 4, 58, 206.
4. *Ibid.*, 307, 413.

replaced Rosecrans with Major General George H. Thomas over the Army of the Cumberland.

Throughout the Chattanooga campaign, Meigs kept both a small pocket diary and several tablets for memoranda of various kinds—orders to subordinates; lists of supplies; plans for depots, boats, and bridges; notes and sketches. He recorded, for instance, a succession of rides in the field, first with Rosecrans and then with Grant, and noted, on November 3, that he had "Moved Hd Quarters into a tent on the Bluff of the River Bend near Gen Grants H Qrs."[5] But most entries are official, not personal, and document his work as an administrator and an engineer. His need for more assistance in these matters evidently prompted Grant to telegraph from Murfreesboro and again from Chattanooga for the services of his son, First Lieutenant John R. Meigs, who had just finished West Point and who was on duty in West Virginia; but Halleck denied the request, which would have left that department without an engineer.[6] Fortunately, the chief engineer in Chattanooga was Brigadier General William F. (Baldy) Smith, who planned and directed the maneuvers shortly after Grant arrived by which the Union opened the "cracker line," a more direct route of supplies by way of the Tennessee and two linking ferries. Meigs reported the ensuing night attack of the Confederates, thwarted by the "valor and steadiness" of the Potomac corps, just as earlier he had reported the first major bombardment of Chattanooga, to which the Cumberland divisions were coolly "indifferent." As Stanton appreciated his dispatches on military actions as well as on supply problems and urged "frequent and full reports," Meigs knew that the government would expect his account of the impending Union offensive. But Grant had to delay an attack until Sherman's army arrived to strengthen the infantry and artillery of Hooker and Thomas. Although the cracker line had saved the troops from starvation, it had not yet provided the forage to avert "the loss of animals," expected by Meigs to "exceed 10,000," and "Those left are scarcely able to carry themselves." For this reason Grant felt an unprecedented "restlessness . . . at the fixed and immovable condition of the Army of the Cumberland."[7]

By November 23, however, the Union command suspected that Bragg had withdrawn his forces between Chattanooga and Missionary Ridge—and indeed he was sending off two divisions to serve with Lieutenant General James Longstreet's corps, already detached to operate against Major General Ambrose E. Burnside's Army of the Ohio in east Tennessee. Thus Bragg was caught off

---

5. Meigs's diary.
6. *O.R.*, I, xxxi, part 1, 774. Correspondence relating to Grant's request will be published in John Y. Simon, ed., *The Papers of Ulysses S. Grant* (Carbondale and Edwardsville, Ill., 1967–), IX (hereafter cited as *PUSG*).
7. *O.R.*, I, xxx, part 4, 102; *ibid.*, I, xxxi, part 1, 774; *ibid.*, I, xxx, part 4, 78; *ibid.*, I, xxxi, part 3, 174, 216.

guard as Grant had Thomas's men advance and secure a new line centered on Orchard Knob about a mile east of town. Meanwhile, Sherman's army arrived, and on November 24 crossed the Tennessee River and struck the Confederate right at the north end of Missionary Ridge. On the same day, Hooker's command moved against the Confederate left on the front slopes of Lookout Mountain, southwest of Chattanooga. This maneuver forced Bragg to evacuate the mountain and to concentrate his troops in defense of the ridge, from Rossville Gap on the south to Tunnel Hill on the north. On November 25, after Hooker was delayed in reaching the former point and Sherman was blocked in several assaults on the latter, Grant ordered Thomas's army against the center. It swept forward and in the last hours of daylight carried the Confederate line not only at the base but also on the crest of the ridge.

Before witnessing this dramatic and decisive defeat of the South, Meigs had gone to Bridgeport, Alabama, to regulate Thomas's principal depot and to meet Sherman's column as it marched toward Chattanooga. According to William W. Smith, who was visiting Grant, Meigs was back for dinner at headquarters on November 20; and when Grant rode forth to observe the three days' battle, he and Smith took turns mounting the "elegant brown horse presented to him by Gen. Meigs." The quartermaster general was a conspicuous figure in the Union command, both at Fort Wood and on Orchard Knob. One observer described him with a "grey beard, a fine looking man of from 50 or 60" (actually 47); another saw him standing among the commanding generals: "There was Meigs, too, smooth, plausible, discreet, and wise."[8]

Meigs shared the troops' euphoria after carrying Missionary Ridge: "The great battle of the Rebellion. . . . a glorious fight . . . a memorable day," he jotted in his diary. Writing also to his father at "nearly one oclock" in the morning, he not only described the events of the day as he did in his journal and his report to Stanton, but stressed his own composure on Orchard Knob: "I felt cool & deliberate & master of my judgmt as though discussing my ordinary business & not excited as some others were." On November 26, he rode over the battlefield from Sherman's crossing to Rossville, "seeing many sad sights" and looking "into the faces of many dead men." Meigs's response was categorical: "The loyal had died the death of heros. . . . The traitors had met a doom lighter than they deserved." His intense feeling on this matter, which generated a lasting bitterness toward the South, was also manifest, for instance, in his picture three weeks before of each side's pickets, who stood

8. *Ibid.*, 162; William Wrenshall Smith, "Holocaust Holiday: The Journal of a Strange Vacation to the War-torn South and a Visit with U. S. Grant," *Civil War Times Illustrated*, XVIII, 6 (Oct., 1979), 32, 33, 35; Christopher Chancellor, ed., *An Englishman in the American Civil War: The Diaries of Henry Yates Thompson* (New York, 1971), 155; [William S. Furay], "Cincinnati 'Gazette' Account" [for Nov. 25, 1863], Frank Moore, ed., *The Rebellion Record* . . . (New York, 1861–69), VIII, Sec. 1, 233.

forty yards apart converse[d] & exchange[d] papers— One waits for the other to starve, & waits in vain— One fights for freedom liberty, governmt, religion & moral order & improvement & the elevation of white & black The other for despotism oppression, to destroy free govrnmt, & retain white & black in the chains of ignorance & prejudice. . . . No rebel foot except as prisoner can again enter Chattanooga.[9]

Meigs remained in the field for a month after this concluding prophecy came true. Although preoccupied with logistical problems, he also traveled about. On November 27 and 28, he caught up with Grant at the front, and was with him when the pursuit of Bragg's army was discontinued for lack of transportation. On November 29, he visited Lookout Mountain and talked with the colonel whose regiment, after the Confederate retreat four nights before, had first reached the summit, unfurling the Union flag at sunrise to the cheers of the armies below. Then in early December, after Sherman's column had departed to relieve Burnside at Knoxville, he joined Grant in a review of the remaining troops and for trips up Lookout, to Tunnel Hill, to Signal Hill north of the river, and to the Chickamauga battlefield. Writing to Stanton from Ringgold, Georgia, he concluded some notes on each side's supply shortages:

This army is relieved from all danger. It will need much to relieve it from all difficulty of transportation & I make my arrangements to keep my head quarters near those of Gen Grant for some time yet. Unless you much need my presence in Washington I should prefer to remain here. The open air life & exercise have been of benefit to me personally. I find my work interesting & useful, & I would not have missed the great battle of Chattanooga for any earthly advantage. It shines among military exploits a diamond of finest lustre.

But Stanton required Meigs's services at the War Department and summoned him back, also denying his request to accompany Grant again in the spring, even though, as Sherman pointed out, a combined army needed a single quartermaster to direct its "vast machinery."[10]

II

By the time Meigs left Tennessee at the end of 1863, his report to Stanton on November 26 was the most widely known account of the battles near Chattanooga, and in time it became almost canonical in Civil War literature.

9. Meigs's diary, Nov. 25; Meigs to his father, Nov. 5, 25 [26]; Meigs's memoranda notebook no. 27, Nov. 26, 1863; and, on Meigs's hostility toward the Confederate states and their leaders, see Russell F. Weigley, *Quartermaster General of the Union Army: A Biography of M. C. Meigs* (New York, 1959), 285–86, 334–36.
10. Meigs's notebook no. 27, Nov. 29, Dec. 1, 2, 5, 9, 10, 1863, and see *O.R.*, I, xxxi, part 2, 162–64; Meigs to Stanton, Nov. 28, 1863, Stanton Papers, Library of Congress; *O.R.*, I, xxxi, part 3, 496, and see *ibid.*, III, iii, 1195; *ibid.*, III, iv, 16; Meigs to Grant, [March] 29, 1864, Gratz Collection, Historical Society of Pennsylvania; *O.R.*, I, xxxii, part 3, 270.

It appeared, for instance, in the *Philadelphia Press* and the *New-York Times* on November 29, and in the *Times* again, the *New-York Tribune*, and the *Boston Evening Traveller* on November 30. Carried (according to Meigs) in "all the newspapers," it also appeared at least twice as a pamphlet and once in a biography of Grant in 1864, and in subsequent accounts of his life it often served as the chapter on Chattanooga or as a summary of the battle.[11] The front-page headlines for Meigs's report usually called it "picturesque" or "graphic," and adapted his phrases, referring for example to "the best-planned" or "the best directed and best ordered" battle of the war. But it was his reference to fighting "above the clouds" that captured most attention. As Hooker's men flanked Lookout on November 24, their compatriots in the plain below watched with intense interest, catching glimpses of the opposing lines when the mists shifted and before rain and darkness fell. Meigs's image doubtless took shape in many minds: "We heard the battle still raging in the clouds above," an English observer remarked, "but we saw no more that afternoon"; by 9:00 P.M., an Ohio soldier was writing of "Hooker's victory above the clouds." But it was Meigs's report, especially as captioned in the Northern press, that gave the phrase general currency. When Lincoln's secretary was asked at a New Year's Eve party about administration policy vis-à-vis the Chase faction in 1864, he replied that it "should be like Hooker's fight at Lookout Mountain, above the clouds."[12]

For a generation, however, writers disputed the accuracy of Meigs's expression. Some participants on each side described the mountain as blanketed by an "impenetrable fog" throughout the day; "literally it was a battle *in* the clouds." In fact, "General Fog commanded on the side of the mountain, while Gen. Hooker commanded in the valley." "There were no clouds to fight above," a *New-York Tribune* correspondent argued, "only a heavy mist." Conversely, a Boston reporter believed that the mist enveloped the summit but not the slopes of the mountain, placing the battle "under the clouds." William F. G. Shanks devised another interpretation, supposing that the fog "over the river" in the morning started to lift during the battle: "Then the smoke of Hooker's musketry and artillery began to mingle with the mist and clouds; they grew heavy again, and settled down close upon the mountain," with the result that he fought "above the clouds of his own making." Although Shanks later elaborated this and other stories of the battle, Grant

11. Meigs's notebook no. 27, Dec. 9, 1863. The separate printings in 1864, in Washington and New York, were each entitled *The Three Days' Battle of Chattanooga* . . . See also Julian K. Larke, *General Grant and his Campaigns* (New York, 1864), 409–12; and, for instance, Henry Coppée, *Grant and his Campaigns: A Military Biography* (New York, 1866), 239–42, and L[oomis] T. Remlap [Palmer], *The Life of General Grant* . . . (Chicago, 1885), 105–11.

12. Chancellor, ed., *Englishman*, 157; Albion W. Tourgée, *The Story of a Thousand: Being a History of the 105th Ohio Volunteer Infantry* . . . (Buffalo, N.Y., 1896), 278; Tyler Dennett, ed., *Lincoln and the Civil War in the Diaries and Letters of John Hay* (New York, 1939), 146.

was said to have found his original account in the *New-York Herald* "very correct." As for Meigs's report, it was also "quite correct as far as it goes."[13]

Meigs's dispatch, especially his account of the battle "above the clouds," evoked a wide literary response, including a number of poems. His own father, an eminent doctor in Philadelphia, composed an "ode" which Meigs copied in his diary, had printed in Chattanooga, and sent to Hooker—a gesture which then prompted the author to send it to *Harper's Weekly*. The battle was also embellished by imaginative writers and artists, largely to Hooker's advantage. Even as the war ended, John W. Geary, one of Hooker's brigadiers (who himself privately claimed to have "stormed" and "captured . . . the impassible and inaccessible heights of Lookout Mountain"), complained that Hooker was "under obligations" to Meigs "for helping him by a single phrase to higher fame than he had ever the chance of winning in any other way. 'Much of Hookers Battle was fought above the clouds which concealed him from our view but from which his musketry was heard' This sentence more than the fight made him famous . . ." It also led to the popular belief that the battle culminated on the crest itself. To the phrase "above the clouds," William Dean Howells added "on the top of Lookout Mountain," and a host of journalists, orators, and regimental historians left the same impression. "The battle of Lookout Mountain," Grant was finally moved to remark, "is one of the romances of the war. There was no such battle, . . . It is all poetry." In a way, Grant was reflecting Sylvanus Cadwallader's contemporary report that the action on November 24 was "in no sense a battle; it was only a long, protracted, magnificent skirmish," and he also may have remembered that Hooker's losses were relatively small while he claimed more prisoners than "the number really captured by the whole army" at Chattanooga. But in another way, Grant's comment, so inflammatory to Hooker's partisans, was a reaction to the exaggerations inspired by Meigs's most quoted phrase, for he later generously described Hooker's "achievement" in rounding the mountain as "brilliant."[14]

The first printings of Meigs's report were badly flawed, causing him much concern and creating difficulty with Sherman. "The telegraph is impossible

13. *O.R.*, I, xxxi, part 2, 691; Charles A. Partridge, ed., *History of the Ninety-Sixth Regiment Illinois Volunteer Infantry* (Chicago, 1887), 269, 272; *New-York Tribune*, quoted in Stanley F. Horn, *The Army of Tennessee* (Indianapolis, 1941), 297; J[ohn] T[ownsend] Trowbridge, *The South: A Tour of its Battle-fields and Ruined Cities . . .* (Hartford, 1866), 257; William F. G. Shanks, *Personal Recollections of Distinguished Generals* (New York, 1866), 175, and see Shanks, "Lookout Mountain, and How We Held It," *Harper's New Monthly Magazine*, XXXVII, 217 (June, 1868), 5, and Shanks, letters in *New-York Daily Tribune*, Aug. 9, 1878, 5, and in *New York Times*, Feb. 12, 1899, part 2, 13; James Harrison Wilson to Adam Badeau, Dec, 11, 1863, Bender Collection, Wyoming State Archives and Historical Department, Cheyenne, Wyo.
14. Meigs's diary, Dec. 6–9, 1863; Meigs to his father, Dec. 5 [6], 1863; [Charles D. Meigs], "Lookout," *Harper's Weekly*, VIII, 367 (Jan. 9, 1864), 22, and see George H. Boker, "The Battle of Lookout Mountain," *Poems of the War* (Boston, 1864), 107–15, and "T. B.," "The

for some news," he explained to his father, "My illegible scrawl for others." Meigs wrote the report "late at night" on November 26, "after a long days ride" along Missionary Ridge. On November 27, eager to join Grant at the front, he handed his manuscript to two assistants and "told them if they could puzzle it out to make a copy" and have it wired to Washington. Their misreadings, and the telegraphers' and typesetters' errors, produced an avalanche of mistakes, two of which Meigs felt compelled to bring to Stanton's attention. The first related to the moon, which shone conspicuously the night of Hooker's battle, especially for the thousands on each side who watched the skirmishing on Lookout Mountain until the Confederates withdrew shortly after midnight. Although many then noted in their diaries and letters the ominous eclipse of the moon, Meigs only mentioned to his father the Napoleonic parallel, which occurred to fewer writers: "[W]e should make the moon of Chattanooga [as] famous as the sun of Austerlitz." In reporting to Stanton, however, his allusion was more homely: "At nightfall the sky cleared, and the full moon, the 'hunter's moon,' shone upon the beautiful scene." As he later explained, the "hunter's moon" of November gave almost as much light as the "harvest moon" of August, but his transcribers, not understanding the reference to the "hunter's moon," changed it to the "traitor's moon" and then to the "traitor's doom." The error persisted, even after Meigs forwarded a correct copy of his report: one biographer of Grant, for instance, referred to the "splendid battle-moon—called by General Meigs, in happy quotation, 'the traitor's doom' . . . "[15]

A second inaccuracy in Meigs's original dispatch, which in itself seemed equally inconsequential, was linked to a view of the battle which tended to slight Sherman's contribution. The technical error, as Meigs informed Stanton, was merely "the ascription to General Thomas of the passage of the Tennessee on our left by General Sherman." As the editor of *Harper's Monthly* hypothesized, this confusion was "purely clerical, owing to obscurity in the Ms., or perhaps to carelessness of proof readers. Sherman and Thomas, when carelessly written, would look very much alike." Meigs regretted the mistake, which "with some will deprive Sherman of the credit due to him." But Meigs had also clearly written that the Army of the Tennessee had been "repulsed"

Battle above the Clouds," Moore, ed., *Rebellion Record*, VIII, Sec. 2, 8–9; Geary to his wife, Dec. 4, 1863, typescript, Chickamauga and Chattanooga National Military Park Library; Meigs to his father, July 24, 1865; Howells, "The Battle in the Clouds," *Poems* (Boston, 1873), 131; John Russell Young, *Around the World with General Grant* (New York, 1879), II, 306; Cadwallader in *Chicago Times*, Dec. 1, 1863, quoted in J. Cutler Andrews, *The North Reports the Civil War* (Pittsburgh, 1955), 482; *O.R.*, I, xxxi, part 2, 325; *Personal Memoirs of U. S. Grant* (New York, 1885–86), II, 539, and see Benjamin P. Thomas, ed., *Three Years with Grant as Recalled by War Correspondent Sylvanus Cadwallader* (New York, 1955), 145–47, and Walter H. Hebert, *Fighting Joe Hooker* (Indianapolis, 1944), 264–65.

15. Meigs to his father, Dec. 8, 1863; *O.R.*, I, xxxi, part 2, 78; Meigs to Stanton, Dec. 11, 1863, Stanton Papers; Coppée, *Grant*, 227.

at Tunnel Hill, even though he believed that its assault, "by calling to that point" the enemy's reserves, "prevented their repulsing any of the others," in particular, Thomas's assault of Bragg's center. Sherman and his friends were quick to fault Meigs, both for the mistaken reference to Thomas and for this view of Tunnel Hill. According to Sherman, the movement there, "seen from Chattanooga, 5 miles off, gave rise to the report, which even General Meigs has repeated, that we were repulsed on the left. Not so: the real attacking columns . . . were not repulsed." Drawing "vast masses of the enemy" to the north end of the ridge, they fought "persistently, stubbornly, and well" until mid-afternoon, when Sherman "felt sure of the result" of Thomas's belated attack. Grant, too, thought that Sherman attracted "the attention of so many of the enemy as to make Thomas' part certain of success." To his brother, Sherman reviewed the matter:

I was provoked that Meigs, looking at us from Chattanooga, should report me repulsed, and that Mr. Stanton should publish his letter as semi-official. Meigs apologized to me for using Thomas's name instead of mine throughout, which he charged to a copyist, but made no amends for the repulse. The whole philosophy of the battle was that I should get, by a dash, a position on the extremity of the Missionary Ridge, from which the enemy would be forced to drive me, or allow his depot at Chickamauga station to be in danger. I expected Bragg to attack me at daylight, but he did not, and to bring matters to a crisis quickly, as time was precious, for the sake of Burnside in East Tennessee, Grant ordered me to assume the offensive.[16]

But Sherman's protestations obscured the unexpected outcome of the battle. Grant's basic plan of attack generally assumed that the Army of the Tennessee would either flank the Confederates or sweep them down the crest of the ridge, and do so before the Army of the Cumberland hit their center. Even in his brief account of the battle, Meigs had touched on a divisive issue within Grant's command. According to Sherman, when he first reached Chattanooga, Grant had explained to him that "the men of Thomas's army had been so demoralized by the battle of Chickamauga that he feared they could not be got out of their trenches to assume the offensive . . ." This opinion, seemingly reflected in the battle plan, stung the Cumberlanders' pride, especially after the publication of Sherman's *Memoirs*, and it may even have spurred them to fight more fearlessly at Missionary Ridge. To Sherman, as to Grant, Meigs, and others on Orchard Knob, they were able to succeed at least partly because

16. Meigs to Stanton, Dec. 11, 1863, Stanton Papers; George William Curtis to Cadwallader, Dec. 27, 1863, Cadwallader Papers, Library of Congress, and see the "Monthly Record of Current Events," *Harper's New Monthly Magazine*, XXVIII, 164 (Jan., 1864), 271; Meigs to his father, Dec. 5 [6], 1863; *O.R.*, I, xxxi, part 2, 45, 78–79, 575–76; William T. Sherman to John Sherman, Dec. 29, 1863, Rachel Sherman Thorndike, ed., *The Sherman Letters: Correspondence between General Sherman and Senator Sherman from 1837 to 1891* (New York, 1894), 217, and see Edward D. Kittoe to Elihu B. Washburne, Dec. 24, 1863, and John E. Smith to Washburne, Jan. 4, 1864, Washburne Papers, Library of Congress.

the veterans of Vicksburg had diverted Bragg's troops from the center to the north end of the ridge. In fact, however, although Bragg from midnight until morning had rushed his divisions from Lookout Mountain on his left to Tunnel Hill on his right, he shifted in midday only a few units for short distances. It was rather the confused and inept defense of the center that enabled Thomas's army to carry the ridge—as can be seen in a series of Confederate battle reports not known to most survivors of the war or to subsequent historians.[17]

Undismayed by the immediate controversy as to whether Sherman's army had set up Thomas's or simply been "repulsed," Meigs sent off a "correct copy" of his initial dispatch, dating it "11¾ P.M." on November 26, but leaving it essentially unchanged. Meanwhile, Stanton appeared oblivious to the dispute, having previously thanked Meigs for a "very interesting report."[18] Ironically, when it was "first correctly printed" in the capital the following year, a new mistake appeared in the title itself, where the battle was dated *23d, 24th, 25th November, 1864.*

III

The following document, Meigs's unpublished "Journal," not only supplements his influential report with information on his own role, but adds substantially to the record of the views of others in the Union command, especially on the final day of battle. While the data on November 23 and 24 are comparable, the journal is much more detailed regarding November 25, causing the manuscript to run over twenty-two pages compared to less than ten in the correct copy of the report. Even in the opening pages, however, the report pares down the story for the sake of dramatic unity: that the Union flag was seen on "the peak of Lookout" at dawn on November 25 is more striking if the two hints that the Confederates would withdraw are omitted; that the Union victory at Missionary Ridge "relieved" Burnside "from danger" instantly anticipates the outcome of the expedition for this purpose—an expedition which was so pressing that Meigs closed his journal for November 24 by noting Grant's plans for it, and which would not even have left Chattanooga if, as Meigs wrote on November 25, Longstreet's army suddenly reappeared in Bragg's lines. Indeed, the report glibly summarizes several important aspects of the final day's battle which are more carefully recorded in the journal. It pictures Hooker's divisions about "to sweep" Missionary Ridge from Rossville Gap, without noting the cannonade at that point with

17. *Memoirs of Gen. W. T. Sherman* (4th ed., New York, 1891), I, 390; John M. Hoffmann, "The Confederate Collapse at the Battle of Missionary Ridge: The Reports of James Patton Anderson and his Brigade Commanders," in preparation; and see Bruce Catton, *Grant Takes Command* (Boston and Toronto, 1969), 77, 91-92, 501n.

18. Meigs to Stanton, Nov. 26, 1863, "True copy," Stanton Papers; *O.R.*, I, xxxi, part 3, 314.

Bragg's left, a signal to Orchard Knob that Thomas's army might soon be sent forward; and it records that Hooker "captured many prisoners," without specifying how the division on Thomas's right took an equal number. The report briefly alludes to Sherman's "assault against Bragg's right," while the journal describes the scene at length, suggesting by its staccato narration how closely and anxiously the battle was viewed from Orchard Knob. Above all, the report merely states, mostly in the passive voice, that a "general advance" of Thomas's army "was ordered," that it followed the Confederates up the sides of the ridge when they abandoned the rifle pits at the base, that "the whole line" was then "ordered to storm the heights," and that it succeeded.[19] Here the journal also reveals Grant's exact directions, his quandary when certain troops, "contrary to orders," started up the hillside, and his willingness "presently" to support them with Thomas's entire force. In fact, neither Grant nor his generals had any idea that the Confederate defense would be so mishandled as to give the Army of the Cumberland the chance to carry the ridge without the immediate assistance of Sherman and Hooker on the flanks. Later commentators reverted to Grant's earlier battle plans and to his subsequent statements to cover Thomas's assault, at least generally, but Meigs, knowing that it exceeded the orders from Orchard Knob, rather chose to phrase his report so as to suppress the most illuminating part of his journal.

The journal, unlike the report, is autobiographical. Meigs was plainly apprehensive about the shelling of Orchard Knob, more so than he appeared or represented to his father. He felt it almost providential that only one member of Grant's staff was hit, and that was on the crest. By that point Meigs had gone up the ridge with Grant and had become a participant himself, attempting to use Confederate cannon against the foe. Although he then helped to reorganize Thomas's men, "wild with excitement," he evidently shared their initial exhilaration upon reaching the crest; at least there is one report that he "busied himself in preparing friction primers for the captured guns which General Grant was ordering into position, but got so excited over the great victory gained that he gave the task up in despair . . ."[20] After returning to Chattanooga, eating a "hearty supper," and reviewing the day at headquarters, he was still so stimulated by the battle as to write about it past midnight. He dashed off the same ideas, even the same phrases, in his diary, his letter home, and his journal, and they recur in later entries and letters and in his report; but the most significant repetition in the following document may be a point made three times: Thomas's army had somehow carried a ridge five hundred feet high.

Meigs wrote the journal in the second of three memoranda notebooks which he kept at Chattanooga. Using a tablet about four inches by seven

19. *Ibid.*, I, xxxi, part 2, 78–79.
20. Shanks, *Personal Recollections*, 119.

inches, he made two or three entries during each day of the battle, judging from his writing and from particular references in different parts of the account. Wanting a clean copy of the main narrative, he then marked the starting point at noon on November 23, ruled off four notes on that day and the next that related to other matters, wrote his initials at the end of November 25, and tore off the bottom of the last sheet—using his third Chattanooga notebook for entries starting on November 26. The only irrelevant passage that he perhaps failed to excise concerned the letters he received from home on November 24. To make his script clear, he inked over several words and phrases. It seems probable that he prepared the manuscript for copying before visiting the battlefield on November 26, that a clerk transcribed it during the day, and that Meigs, when he wrote his report to Stanton that night, had before him his contemporaneous record of the fighting—not in the crabbed hand of memoranda notebook no. 22, but in the legible script of the "Journal of the Battle of Chattanooga. November 23d. 24th. & 25th 1863" (the title appearing in capital letters on the cover and the first page of the copy). Meigs had thus jotted down a running narrative of the fighting from which he could then fashion a single report, more concise and more "literary" than his initial account.

The following text is an exact transcription of the copy because Meigs's own writing is at many points undecipherable, especially without reference to the copy. The copyist altered various details of capitalization and punctuation, spelled out ampersands, inserted paragraphs, put Orchard Knob in quotes, and turned Missionary Ridge into Mission Ridge, the older name. But these changes are inconsequential. Meigs himself carefully reviewed and corrected the copy, and signed the initials of his name and rank at the end. He kept the document among his papers, writing on the cover a cross, the date "Nov. 21. 1879," and a bit of shorthand: as his wife died on that day, he apparently thought of her loss while leafing through his Civil War records. Meigs died in 1892, and in 1944 his granddaughter added the journal to the Meigs Papers in the Library of Congress. It has not been published except for excerpts, including a few sentences in biographies of Meigs and of Grant, and a longer passage in *The Papers of Ulysses S. Grant.*[21] It appears here in its entirety, both to complement Meigs's well-known report to Stanton and to throw new light on Grant and his command at Chattanooga.

JOURNAL OF THE BATTLE OF CHATTANOOGA
Nov. 23d. 24th & 25. 1863.

At noon November 23rd 1863 a demonstration ordered to develope the enemy on Mission Ridge.

21. Weigley, *Quartermaster General*, 290; Catton, *Grant Takes Command*, 83–84; forthcoming in *PUSG*, IX.

Rode to Fort Wood[22] with Grants Head Quarters.

At 2 P.M. skirmishers opened on the rebel pickets all along the line, and drove them in with sharp interchange of musketry.

Our troops advanced steadily in line of battle, and drove the rebels from a long line of rifle-pits, and crowned "Orchard Knob" and the low ridge to the right of it, and formed on that front.

Some two hundred prisoners, I judge, were brought in, some [Union] men of course were wounded and some, I fear, killed, though no reports have come in.

Two Alabamians were the first brought in, very much excited and very stupid. Did not know the name of their Brigade Commanders, but said Hindman's Division, to which they belonged were all here.[23]

At 3½ P.M. Gen. Grant was back in his quarters, writing his despatches.

The Artillery firing from Fort Wood continues—shelling, I suppose the rebel Camps and works on Mission Ridge, and endeavoring to prevent any massing against our troops in the advance.

General Thomas reports to night 169 prisoners, Alabamians, our loss not yet reported.

Bridges both broken "Dunbar" ferrying at Chattanooga—Mule Boat at Brown's Ferry—Woods Division still waiting to cross at Brown's Ferry.[24]

Fort Wood Chattanooga
24th November 1863. A.M.

Dropping fire among the pickets in front—Troops resting on their arms since daylight—since I have been here.

Visited the lines and watched the battle from various parts of the field. The principal fighting to day was on the nose of Lookout Mountain which General Hooker carried—He rests to the left of the White [Craven's] House holding the cleared ground.

His Camp fires show to night, and picket firing continues. General Sherman crossed above us, and is established on the south side of the River—expects to carry point of Mission Ridge before he rests for the night.

Howard moved up South Bank of the River and effected a junction with Sherman and returned, leaving him a Brigade and posting another half way. The Dunbar towed up two flats and crossed some 6000 troops during the day. She has been of essential service. Granger, Sheridan and Baird [commanding parts of Thomas's army] rested in the position seized and fortified yesterday.

The enemy has not to us shown himself in force, except on Lookout, where he

22. Fort Wood was the major salient of the Union line on the east side of Chattanooga, less than half a mile from town.
23. Most of the 28th Alabama Infantry was captured near Orchard Knob. It was part of Brig. Gen. Arthur M. Manigault's brigade, with which it also fought at Chickamauga. *O.R.*, I, xxxi, part 2, 251, 659; *ibid.*, I, xxx, part 2, 15.
24. Because Brig. Gen. Charles R. Woods's division of Sherman's army was unable to cross into Chattanooga, Grant ordered it to report to Hooker, who was thereby authorized to move against Lookout Mountain. *Ibid.*, I, xxxi, part 2, 32, 42, 105, 106-7, 314.

resisted Hooker and stood at last checking his advance. His wagons were seen coming down the Summertown Road which looks like abandoning the Mountain.[25]

Letters from my wife and children by Mr. Freas the Carpenter, who arrived during the day.

11 P.M. Point of Lookout Mt. and the N. E. Hill of Mission Ridge are ablaze with Camp fires of Hooker and Sherman. Rest of both Ridges dark. Bright moonlight— clear North wind—General attack or advance ordered for daybreak. Picket firing seems to have ceased—Rebels have probably evacuated.

And now to bed—I have just returned from Gen. Grant's, Granger will, if the rebels have run, march to-morrow with 20,000 men to relieve Burnside beseiged in Knoxville. Steamer "Paint Rock" will follow him with provisions.

> Chattanooga 25th Nov. 1863
> Woods Fort 7. A.M.

Sun appeared just above Mission Ridge—Large bodies of troops moving to our left along the summit gaining a position on the high point.[26]

American flag waving from the top of the rock at N. E. end of Lookout Mt. Our troops apparently in possession—no firing.

Clear beautiful morning, smoke and mist hang in the valleys summit clear.

We shall have a battle on Mission Ridge.

Gen. Howard with whom I rode to Woods redoubt parted with me there, and I remained until Mr. C. A. Dana, Asst. Secy. War came up and proposed that we should pay Granger's Head Quarters a visit.

I told him I was waiting for Genl. Grant, near whom I wished to be during the day. But concluding that we could ride to "Orchard Knob" and return by the time any serious movement would be made—I consented to visit Granger.

We found Gen. Wood—Granger was visiting his lines—Gave him the information that the flag waved on Lookout Crest (From wounded prisoner I have since learned that Stevenson evacuated the Mountain about 1 A.M. the night previous.) This was good news to him—Hooker had orders to move to join in a general advance upon the rebel lines.

We rode to the "Orchard Knob" henceforth historical, and there remained 'till Gen. Grant was seen approaching. The first salutation I had on the Knob was from a Rifled piece—a 10 pdr. on the summit of Mission Ridge opposite, which sent a shell whizzing, exploding and sputtering, and dropping its butt into a hole some fifteen feet in front of the group of Gen. W. F. Smith, Major Dana and myself—An officer who saw it fall, I was not looking up being occupied in reading some letters from home, picked it up and handed it to me.

A battery of these 10 pdrs. rifled fired at the "Knob" all day. Head Quarters

25. Hooker encircled the "nose" of Lookout Mountain, immediately below the Point, the northern promontory of the mountain, about a thousand feet above the valley floor. The Summertown road ran down the eastern side of the mountain, leaving the crest about a mile south of the Point.

26. At this time, the Confederates who had been withdrawn from Lookout Mountain were wending their way along Missionary Ridge to Tunnel Hill. From Fort Wood, however, they may have appeared to have only reached the spur later known as DeLong Point.

remained there 'till about 4 P.M., and every few minutes throughout the day, a shell whizzed past the Knob on which stood Generals Grant, Thomas, Granger, Wood, W. F. Smith, Rawlings [Rawlins] myself and a crowd of officers of the Staff. No one was hit near us, however, and it was not until Mission Ridge or part of it was carried that any officer of General Grant's Staff was hit. Lt. Towner, when dispatched at my request that some officer should be sent back to bring up artillerists to work against the enemy some of the guns captured on the Heights was shot through the back of the neck and shoulder within a minute after leaving us to execute the order—All others escaped.

The day wore on—cannonade at Sherman's position fortified on the left Knobs of Mission Ridge, and much musketry continued, Orchard Knob replied to the guns on the Ridge, other Batteries to the right joined in the chorus. Woods redoubt with its 30 pdr Parrotts and its 4½" guns sent shell screaming over us towards the guns on Mission Ridge—Occasionally guns to the right and left of our front on Mission Ridge would open but the only rifled guns seemed to be those directly in front of us, and they alone had range to reach us, and they fired at intervals all day, and we were the conspicuous mark. Occasionally they would drop a shell into our picket, or rather skirmish line, which advanced early in the day, and drove in the rebel pickets.

The day wore away, I was impatient at the delay—night was approaching, and so might be Longstreet, recalled from Burnsides front at Knoxville.

A cannonade at Rossville Gap at last opened, It was of short duration. It was Hooker who had descended the Lookout[27] Mountain and crossed the valley and attacked two Regiments and a section of Artillery guarding the pass. A wagon train loading with flour and the troops and Artillery escaped him and the sound died away.

A line was seen deployed in a cleared field on Sherman's right—a blue line which went steadily up the steep ascent. Soon another followed in support. How gallant an assault, It is impossible for them to succeed were the exclamations. I watched them with my telescope, an excellent one, saw them pass the fence at the upper edge of the field, enter the oak woods, climb to the edge of the crest of the hill, whose profile is thus:[28] and stop   A sputtering musketry fire broke out. The men sought shelter from the deadly fire of the log breast-work above them. I saw the reserve brought up to resist the assault, filling the terrepleine of the entrenchment[29] with a mass of gray. I saw officers leaping into the air and waving their swords urging and calling their rebel soldiers to the front. I saw the reserve fall back again out of fire.

I saw a great body of troops move from a Camp between our front and Sherman and pass steadily along the ridge to assist in repelling the assault. I saw the men again urged forward slowly, step, first a few, then more, then the whole body over the breast-works, and advance pouring their fire into our men, who stood fast and returned it.

Then the rebels nearer to us advanced and taking our men crowded under shelter of the hills in flank, poured into them a murderous fire, and the right flank of the group dissolved, and the open field below was filled with men running down the hill. The

27. Evidently to avoid confusion, Meigs inserted the word "Lookout" at this point.
28. The copyist here drew what he called a "Section of Mission Ridge." As in Meigs's sketch, he showed the sides tapering off at about a 45-degree angle, but he also added a flat crest between the slopes.
29. The terreplein was the horizontal embankment or platform just behind the parapet.

rebels cast stones from their rifle pits into our men thus wounding some, so near were the two hostile bodies during the half hour or hour that they thus stood in deadly array before the rebel charge.

Our men at last gave way, and fled down the hill and through the field in confusion.

Colonel Putnam, Commanding an Illinois Regiment whom I had noticed, riding a brown horse, leading his men up the slope, difficult for a horse to climb, was shot through the head.[30] A Major who gallantly urged a black charger up the hill, escaped the storm unhurt.

General Grant repeated his order for a general advance, now making it an order that all the troops in sight should advance, drive back the rebel pickets and following them closely, run them into and over their breast-works, which solidly constructed of logs and earth, extended in nearly continuous lines for two miles along the base of the Ridge.

The troops were impatient for work. They were formed; a strong line of skirmishers, a line of battle deployed behind them:—the signal six cannon shots from "Orchard Knob" was given and forward they sprang with a cheer. With a quick step not a run, they[31] crossed the space between us and the breastworks. The rebels fired a volley, our men fired at will, and the rebels swarming out of the rifle-pits covered the lower slopes behind them turned to look at our advance and firing a few shots, again turned and swarmed up the steep roads, which, by oblique ascents led to the summit.

Mission Ridge is 500 feet high its sides nearly denuded of timber cut for Camp fires but still with many oaks upon the slopes.

The order was to form on our side of the breast-works, and then send a regiment or two to wheel to the right and sweep the rebels out of their works and capture as many as possible.

Every gun on Mission Ridge broke out with shell and shrapnell upon the heads of our gallant troops, who never halted till they reached the breastworks.

Most of them halted there; but the colors of three Regiments pushed on and up the slopes of a projecting spur, too steep to be seen from the summit.[32] Mission Ridge is here five hundred feet in height. Slowly the three red silken flags ascended and the regiments swarmed up after them.

General Grant said it was contrary to orders, it was not his plan—he meant to form the lines and then prepare and launch columns of assault, but, as the men; carried away by their enthusiasm had gone so far, he would not order them back.

Presently he gave the order for the whole line, now well formed to advance and storm the ridge. It extended some two miles in length, and it pressed forward with cheers. Shot and shell and cannister poured into it right and left, our guns, 10 pdr rifles, on "Orchard Knob" responded firing into the batteries, exploding a caisson,[33] and disturbing the gunners.

---

30. O.R., I, xxxi, part 2, 653.
31. The words "pressed forward" appear in Meigs's notebook at this point; the copyist overlooked them and Meigs did not notice the omission.
32. This part of the ridge was probably the DeLong Point, defended by Brig. Gen. Zachariah C. Deas's brigade.
33. Meigs evidently corrected the copyist by inserting the second "s" in this word.

The line ceased to be a line. The men gathered towards the points of least difficult ascent, for very steep is this hill-side, a horse cannot ascend or descend except by the obliquely graded roads. The three colors approach the summit, another mass, gathered gradually into a confused column or stream, at another point directly, in our front, reaches the summit, the color bearer springs forward and plants his flag upon the crest, a gun gallops wildly to the right, cheer upon cheer rings out from actors and spectators.[34] The men swarm up, color after color reaches the summit, and the rebel line is divided and the confused, astonished and terrified rebels fly this way and that to meet enemies, every way but down the rear slope of the ridge and by this open way they mostly escape.

Bragg whose Head Quarters are in a house in plain sight to the right of our front, astonished at our success leaves the house, passing from the porch through and out the back door, mounts his horse and rides down the hill-side. Our men then crowned the summit, and had they known it, could by a volley, have put an end to this traitors career, as he fled down the road.

Still, between Sherman and Baird, whose division made the left assault, remained a mile of fortified ridge, held by the rebels. Fierce musketry broke out on the summit, for the "unpainted house" guns still blazed each way and Gen. Grant determined to go to the summit, and see that proper order was restored.[35]

I rode with him, soon found three brass pieces, a limber and caisson; but no lanyard and no artillery-men—the cartridges near the piece piled at its wheel were round shot—I directed some of the men [who were] lying down behind the rebel breastwork looking to see Bairds line formed across the ridge and hotly engaged give way, while still from the right, at the unpainted house, the cannon blazed,—to bring the limber and caissons behind the breastworks, had the chests examined, found friction tubes and shell, but no lanyard with which to discharge them.[36] An ordnance officer heard me asking for primers and said he had some in his saddle bags. He always carried them and sometimes found them very useful.

The suspension hook from my own and a Captains sword-belt, we wrenched off for hooks, a piece of bed cord, which I found on the ground, completed the Lanyard, and the guns were turned into a battery and ready for use. Gen. Baird spoke to me. I asked Gen. Grant to send back for artillerists and lanyards, and he sent Lt. Towner, who was wounded as he left us.[37]

Gen. Baird requested me to ride with him to the left, now the front, where the musketry roared and raged. We spoke to every officer, many men, wild with excitement—color bearers seeking their Colonels and men their colors—urged the necessity

34. Although Meigs first noted the three flags of the soldiers nearing the DeLong Point, he reported here the initial break in the Confederate line in a section between the Shallow Ford and Bird's Mill roads that had been assigned to Brig. Gen. James Patton Anderson's brigade, commanded by Col. William F. Tucker.

35. Although Thomas's army rather quickly cleared the crest of Anderson's division, units of Lt. Gen. William J. Hardee's corps held the ground to the north until dark. One point of resistance in the other direction was near the "unpainted house," possibly as far south as Brig. Gen. William B. Bate's division.

36. The last dashes and bracketed words in this sentence have been inserted to clarify Meigs's apparent meaning.

37. Meigs here crossed out the word "me" and inserted the word "us," which appears in his notebook.

of forming the men at once and that Bragg's army might still by a charge sweep us from the Ridge. Got a line formed across the ridge in the rear of the one so hotly engaged. Set the men to carrying the logs of the rebel-breastworks to the rear edge of the narrow summit, and to forming barricades of timber across the summit. Rode up to the front line and finding that the answer from the part of the hill in rebel possession was dying out, stopped the firing, ordered a breastwork and that the men should lie down behind it, and not fire unless attacked. Ordered a discreet officer and a patrol to be sent out to ascertain what was in front, and finding order being restored and troops regularly organized into bodies which could be handled, marching into position, as it became dark, I, with Gen. Wilson[38] of the Engrs, who had joined me, bade Baird good-night, and rode to my tent.

It was dark as we turned away—the moon just then showed her face above the range, and late I reached my tent—ate a hearty supper and went to Hd Qrs to hear the result.

Hooker came in, reported that we had captured 2000 prisoners on Lookout and 1000 on Mission Ridge, and that Johnson's Division had captured a thousand.

Four thousand to Five thousand prisoners, thirty five guns and many small arms are the trophies. The substantial results are not yet known. Burnside will be relieved at once. Two steam boats arrived at our wharf from Bridgeport during the fight, Hooker having raised the blockade yesterday.

Bragg with a beaten and discontented army in full retreat, burning and destroying behind him. Invasion of Kentucky and Tennessee indefinitely postponed.

The Slave aristocracy broken down. The grandest stroke yet struck for our country.

Our loss is small considering the exploit. The storming of a steep hill five hundred feet high on a front of two miles, every where doubly entrenched by a line of troops which soon lost their formation and streamed upward, aggregating into channels as a sheet of water would have done in descending the same hill. It is unexampled— Another laurel leaf is added to Grant's Crown.

M C MEIGS
Q M Gn
U S A[39]

---

38. Meigs here crossed out the word "late," evidently recalling that Brig. Gen. James H. Wilson would have retained his regular appointment in the army corps of engineers even though he served on Grant's staff at this point as assistant inspector general.
39. Meigs himself here signed his name and position.

VI

Samuel H. Beckwith
"Grant's Shadow"

Edited by John Y. Simon
and David L. Wilson

Introduction

The use of the telegraph for military purposes constituted one of the technological revolutions in warfare during the Civil War. This rapid communication network had a decided impact on Civil War strategy and tactics, since commanders could move armies and direct battles from a distance. Information about supplies, enemy movements, and troop positions was often no farther away than the nearest telegraph office. Alert telegraph operators also often provided news of events within hours or even minutes of their occurrence.[1]

Although it took some months to organize a military telegraph system, Union authorities appreciated the significance of the telegraph from the very beginning of the conflict. On May 20, 1861, the government seized the previous year's backfiles in all the principal commercial telegraph offices under Union control to see what messages had been transmitted by ringleaders in the secession movement.[2] Anson Stager, appointed a colonel in the Quartermaster Department, assumed control of the military telegraph system on November 21. Because telegraph operators were usually civilians under contract to the government and directly responsible to Stager, not to local military commanders, friction often resulted. In this way, however, the War Department maintained direct control over a rapidly growing communications network which

---

1. For accounts of the military telegraph system, see David Homer Bates, *Lincoln in the Telegraph Office* (New York, 1907); William R. Plum, *The Military Telegraph during the Civil War in the United States* (Chicago, 1882); U.S. Senate, Committee on Pensions, *Relief of Telegraph Operators who Served in the War of the Rebellion*, 58th Cong., 2d sess., April 7, 1904, S. Doc. 251.
2. Plum, I, 69.

eventually included over 15,000 miles of telegraph lines. The key to the efficiency of this vast network was the telegraphers.

The telegraphers were an unusual group. Before the Civil War many seem to have been largely without roots, drifting from town to town as new jobs and opportunities opened up. They were technicians, not generally well-educated, and did not normally associate with the upper levels of society. Their low social status contrasted with the importance that they assumed during the war. The staff of general officers they served consisted of educated elites—a clear distance was maintained between officers and men. Given the nature of their position, however, the telegraphers became the confidants of the great and powerful, giving them a unique perspective on the war as they were often the first to know what was happening. And they had an enormous responsibility because a minor error in telegraphy could produce military disaster.[3]

Ulysses S. Grant understood—as did many other field commanders—the value of the telegraph for directing military operations.[4] With the exception of the Vicksburg campaign when he was not in direct telegraphic communication with the outside world, Grant relied constantly on the telegraph to keep his superiors informed, for information about enemy movements, and as a means of instructing his subordinates.[5] From early in the war, the bulk of Grant's military correspondence was carried over telegraph lines rather than through the mails.

As Grant's importance as a military commander increased, it became imperative to provide him with a secure means of telegraphic communication, since Confederates constantly slipped through Union defenses to tap telegraph lines. Hence Grant needed a secure cipher that could not be broken by Confederates in the event that they intercepted any of his messages. A cipher was developed solely for his use and only his cipher operator was allowed access to it.[6] This even included Grant's personal staff officers. Grant normally wrote out his telegrams in longhand for encoding and transmission by his cipher clerk and telegrapher. His operator, Samuel H. Beckwith, was usually the first to know what was on Grant's mind. He was also the first to know what was being sent to Grant over the wires because it was his responsibility to decode the messages. Again, accuracy in both directions was essential.

Beckwith had enlisted as a private in Company F, 11th Illinois, on July 30, 1861, and participated in the battles of Fort Donelson and Shiloh. When not fighting, he often worked as an assistant telegrapher. He was discharged from the 11th Illinois on February 19, 1863, to assume duties as telegraph and cipher operator for Grant. Because of his good work, Grant recommended him for a commission in the Army Signal Corps on November 8; Beckwith, however, remained a civilian employee of the U.S. Military Telegraph. Since he was the only person who knew the cipher, Beckwith had to be Grant's constant companion. With two brief exceptions, he went everywhere Grant did, sometimes gaining insights into Grant's character, especially the emotional

---

3. A reading of Plum and of Bates provides the basis for this analysis.

4. *Personal Memoirs of U. S. Grant* (New York, 1885-86), II, 103-4, 205-7.

5. Grant used the telegraph heavily during the siege of Vicksburg to keep in touch with various headquarters on the siege lines. However, there was no secure telegraph line connecting Grant with the North. Hence Grant would send messages by steamboat to be transmitted to Washington, or elsewhere, from Memphis or Cairo. This process would often take a week or more.

6. For an illustration of the cipherbook of Samuel H. Beckwith, see Bates, 57.

side, not readily apparent to others. Beckwith was also associated briefly with President Abraham Lincoln at the close of the war and later was involved in the capture of John Wilkes Booth. With the exception of some minor errors, his account appears to be reliable.

Beckwith published several accounts of his Civil War services with Grant in newspaper and magazine articles. An interview of Beckwith entitled "Lincoln in Richmond"[7] described his assignment to Lincoln from March 25–April 6, 1865, while the president visited Grant at City Point, Virginia. His assignment to Lincoln revealed Grant's trust in the abilities of his telegrapher. During Lincoln's visit, the Confederate lines around Petersburg collapsed and Richmond fell, leading to Lincoln's visit to the captured Confederate capital. An abbreviated version of Beckwith's story was printed in the New York *Times*, May 31, 1914. The following account, the most extensive version, appeared in the Sunday magazine of the New York *Sun* in four installments, April 6–27, 1913. Beckwith's articles were edited by William Ross Lee, an attorney of Utica, New York. An article written earlier by Beckwith alone suggests that Lee's literary contribution was substantial.[8] Beckwith received a pension for substantial damage to his eyesight while a wartime telegrapher, another indication that he needed assistance in preparing his "Memoirs."

The following text appears as printed in the New York *Sun*. Introducing the series, Lee wrote that "Capt. Beckwith is now a resident of Utica, N. Y., and is 74 years old. During the War of the Rebellion he possessed the confidence and respect of Gen. Grant to an unlimited degree, and next to that commander himself he held all the most important secrets of the campaigns of the years 1862–1865." Beckwith died in a soldiers' home in Hampton Roads, Virginia, December 7, 1916.[9]

MEMOIRS OF GRANT'S SHADOW

Reminiscences of Samuel H. Beckwith, Gen. U. S. Grant's Telegrapher and Cipher Operator, 1862–65

To write interestingly of men and of incidents of the civil war period of our history fifty years after that momentous conflict has ended would seem a well nigh impossible task; such a volume of narration has been published of its battles and sieges and marches and hardships. Many of the generals who were prominent in the struggle have described ably and elaborately the campaigns in which they participated, and a score of lesser lights, whose parts in the great drama afforded them peculiar means of knowledge, have given their reminiscences to the public. It may be that there is a surfeit of such literature. My excuse for writing these memoirs is the belief that I have treated a trite theme in a new way; have seldom traversed familiar ground, and have told

---

7. Unidentified clipping, Ulysses S. Grant Association, Carbondale, Ill.
8. Samuel H. Beckwith, "Silhouettes by 'Grant's Shadow': Personal Reminiscences of Famous Union Generals and Statesmen," *National Magazine (Boston)*, XX (Aug., 1904), 562–73; see also a speech by Beckwith reminiscing about Grant's staff officer Ely S. Parker printed in "Marking the Grave of Do-ne-ho-geh-weh," *Proceedings of the Buffalo Historical Society*, VIII (1905), 514–19.
9. New York *Times*, Dec. 8, 1916.

only what I have seen and heard. And I have had exceptional opportunity of seeing and hearing.

It was shortly after the battle of Corinth, which was fought on the 3d and 4th days of October, 1862, that I was transferred to Gen. U. S. Grant to fill the position of telegraph operator. I had enlisted as a private in Company F, Eleventh Illinois Infantry, May 9 of the same year[10] for three months service; and had reenlisted for three years as sergeant, receiving the appointment of private secretary to Col. (afterward Major-Gen.) W. H. L. Wallace, who was killed at Shiloh. My clerical duties had brought me into contact with Grant, who was at that time brigade commander in charge of the Southwestern Missouri District;[11] and I had come to admire this quiet, energetic soldier, who scorned display and braggadocio. It was with genuine satisfaction, therefore, that I received the news of my assignment to him; and my knowledge of telegraphy was such that I felt secure in my new place.

It was now that my long period of usefulness under him began, a period of almost three years of constant intimacy, during which I retained, I am proud to say, his unvarying confidence and friendship. I am sure that I am guilty of no misstatement of fact when I assert that very few men were so fortunately situated as I to know well the great Federal leader while he was with the army. From this time on, until he put aside the sword to take up the peaceful pursuits of the citizen I was, with the exception of perhaps two weeks, his ever present attendant, at his beck and call at all hours of the day and night. After I became his cipher operator in 1863 we were necessarily inseparable; for, depending solely upon me to translate into readable English all of his important dispatches, he was obliged to take me with him wherever he went. No staff officer, with possibly the exception of Rawlins, was so indispensable to him; and this is not egotism but the simple truth. My position made me indispensable.

It is consequently from a rich store of information that I am able to write these memoirs.

I. With Grant at Vicksburg.

Pemberton's army had been effectually bottled up behind the intrenchments at Vicksburg, and the lines of the Union forces, under the admirable direction of their general, had rendered by their impregnable offence the surrender of the Confederates imperative. It had been a long and tedious task. Since the middle of May we had been hammering away at the stubborn enemy with varying success; now rushing the defenders with energetic assault, only to be beaten back with great losses; now, realizing the futility of such an attack,

---

10. Actually 1861.
11. On Aug. 28, 1861, Grant was assigned to command of the District of Southeast Mo. and later located his headquarters at Cairo, Ill. See John Y. Simon, ed., *The Papers of Ulysses S. Grant* (Carbondale and Edwardsville, Ill., 1967–), II, 151, 163 (hereafter cited as *PUSG*).

creeping slowly and surely toward the formidable works by the uninspiring process of sapping and mining and the other hard drudgery of the siege. Before victory crowned our efforts, we had 75,000 men before the intrenched camp of our opponents, who numbered approximately 30,000; but the strength of those hostile fortifications almost counterbalanced this inequality of numbers.

I do not propose to tax the reader's patience with a rehearsal of the well known details of the historic operations about Vicksburg. Gen. Grant himself has written fully upon this interesting subject, and I am not competent to add anything to what he has said. It is only of the final chapter of the campaign that I wish to speak, some of the incidents of which have not yet been fully and accurately described. I occupied a tent within a stone's toss of headquarters during those seven weeks of southern summer weather and, in the performance of my duties as telegrapher I saw much of events that was denied to the troops in the trenches.

On July 4, 1863, at 3 o'clock in the morning, Pemberton's acceptance of the terms which had been submitted to him but a few hours before was received by Grant, and soon afterward the General came to my tent and aroused me from a restless doze into which I had lapsed while awaiting news of the capitulation. In the dim candle light, his eyes looked very tired and his face wan and drawn, but he greeted me with a pleasant smile as he said:

"Well, Beckwith, Pemberton has accepted our terms and will surrender at 9 o'clock in the morning. Now can you raise Sherman?"

While he leaned for support against the centre pole I opened the key and called for Butler, Sherman's operator. As I subsequently learned, this faithful fellow was sleeping at quarters, with his head pillowed in a cracker box, on the top of which he had placed his little instrument. I had sounded the call scarcely ten seconds when the welcome click of Butler's reply fell like music upon my ears.

"Hold on a minute until I get a light," he demanded.

"Have you got him?" asked Grant.

I nodded my head and he gave me a written order that he held in his hand, addressed to Gen. Sherman. It directed him to move at daylight and announced the surrender of the Confederates.

While I was sending the message, he stood interestedly by my side, and as soon as I was done, he bade me good night and retired, I suppose to catch a few hours of much needed rest. When he was gone, I ticked off the signal "23," which signified in our code language that I had news for the whole army. Then I flashed the welcome intelligence around the entire line, from Warrenton to Haynes' Bluff, and for a few moments the wires hummed a jubilant thanksgiving. It was information for which the boys had been waiting these many long days, and it filled their hearts, I dare say, with "exceeding great joy." It was, I know, with a feeling of intense happiness that I put out my light and threw myself upon my cot to dream of the dawn of peace.

Shortly before 9 o'clock on that memorable day, Gen. Grant, with staff and escort mounted, rode out midway between the great defensive lines of earthworks and rested in the saddle. I accompanied the little party and was a witness of the last act of the drama. The morning was hot and sultry and it required mighty small exertion to start beads of perspiration trickling down the face. Along the parapets of the Federal works the Union soldiers crowded, eager watchers of the scene that must have aroused in them the deepest emotions. It meant a surcease, at least for a time, of privation and hardships and toil and dangers; and it meant also a successful culmination of a most strenuous campaign.

From the sally ports before us they came out by regiments, 30,000 men who had fought the good fight and succumbed at last to superior prowess and numbers, stacked their arms and retired again to their own lines, prisoners of war. Not a cheer went up from the thousands of Federal troops who were spectators of the surrender; with a charity that was worthy of our best traditions, they maintained a silence that was doubtless, balm to the wounded pride of their defeated foe. It was all done with despatch. We were now privileged to enter those portals that had long been barred to our approach.

I was glad when these formalities were concluded, for it was becoming exceedingly warm and breathing was by no means a pleasure in that atmosphere. The tramping of myriads of feet had stirred up a fine, yellow clay dust that coated our garments and filled our eyes and ears and nostrils until it was almost unbearable. With the passage of the last of the Confederates from the field Grant and his escort rode within the abandoned works and gazed about them at the marks of our incessant bombardment, which were manifest upon every side. I wondered at the fortitude of the enemy in holding out so stoutly against what must have seemed to them inevitable defeat. Certainly the cessation of hostilities was timely because a prolongation of the conflict under the circumstances was utterly useless.

We had ridden perhaps half a mile when we reined up on what at some time or other might have been a pretty and well kept lawn, but which now was overgrown with long grass and weeds. It faced an old fashioned Southern mansion that looked out over the waste like some luckless wight who overborne by misfortune surveys the wreck of his hopes. Evidently the war had called away those who were charged with its care and maintenance. On the left side of this venerable building were large double parlors, with two full length windows opening out upon a piazza, about which ran a low ornamental iron railing.

We dismounted, and Grant, unattended, ascended the broad front steps, some ten in number. As he reached the piazza Gen. Pemberton emerged from one of the front windows and stood for a single moment glaring upon his conqueror. Then without any salutation he abruptly turned half way around and from just inside the window lifted out his sword, with belt and revolver officially wrapped about it. The hilt he thrust more than offered to his opponent, and at the same time murmured some words which I couldn't understand, although I was standing scarcely ten feet away. Grant placed his hand delicately upon the proffered sword and said:

"Retain your side arms, General."

For several seconds a somewhat embarrassing silence ensued, as neither commander, apparently, could find suitable words for expression. From his attitude I am inclined to believe that the Confederate leader was perfectly willing to dispense with all civilities; but Grant was determined to play the gentleman. He pulled out his cigar case and extended it to Pemberton, who after a momentary hesitancy and as if the effort cost him some self-respect gingerly selected a weed. The former took one also and both lighted up, an act which ordinarily is a precursor of a better acquaintance; but which, in this instance, seems to have had no beneficial effect.

What remarks passed between them now I don't know. I was dusty and weary from my ride and anxious for some relief, so with several of the officers I left the leaders to themselves and gave myself over to our host's (?) corps of body servants, who, by generous ministrations of water and towels and brush brooms, restored us to normal condition.

Gen. Pemberton's treatment of his humane adversary was unworthy of the boasted chivalry of the South. He appeared to harbor a sullen animosity toward the man whose initiative had caused the downfall of his army, and his churlish response to Grant's courtesy impressed me at the time as being both petty and unsoldierly. This conduct, so we are told, he persisted in during the final arrangements of the terms of surrender, and his staff supported him in his boorish behavior.

It is but fair to the South, however, to say that Pemberton was not a native of Dixie. He was a Pennsylvanian by birth and a West Point graduate, the only Northerner who was given high command on the Confederate side.[12] Jefferson Davis had been vigorously criticised for appointing him to a place of such considerable responsibility, not only because he was from the North, but because he held the rank of Major only in the service of the United States, and was, therefore, comparatively untried and untested.

Pollard in his history of "The Lost Cause" describes Pemberton as an officer "of a captious and irritable nature, a narrow mind, the slave of the forms and fuss of the schools, whose idea of war began with a bureau of clothing and ended with a field day or dress parade."[13]

If this be true, possibly it explains in part his lack of gallantry toward Gen. Grant, but there certainly can be no valid excuse for such ungenerous conduct.

---

12. Beckwith is incorrect on this point; see Charles M. Cummings, *Yankee Quaker Confederate General: The Curious Career of Bushrod Rust Johnson* (Rutherford, N.J., 1971).
13. The wording is slightly different, but the meaning is the same in Edward A. Pollard, *The Lost Cause . . .* (New York, 1866), 387.

II. As Cipher Operator.

In the month of September, 1863, I was appointed cipher operator or cryptographer to Gen. Grant, and thenceforward I accompanied him personally during his campaigns, having exclusive charge of his cipher correspondence. So much has been written about the cipher corps and codes in recent years that an extended reference to either of them would be a needless expenditure of time. I will make therefore only passing comment.

Anson Stager, David H. Bates, Charles Tinker and Albert B. Chandler were employed at the War Department at Washington as cipher constructors, if I may so use the word. It was their business to devise suitably complex and incomprehensible codes so as to baffle any curious enemy into whose hands a message might fall. The key to the cipher code was given of course to the operator. Naturally the success of the code depended upon its non-solvability by any one except the man in possession of the key, and that non-solvability was a characteristic of these codes can be readily inferred from the following paragraph which I take from my scrap book, an extract from an article in the *Telegraph Age* of September 16, 1898:

"Arbitrary words were used to represent proper names and also many ordinary words and military phrases. The words of the entire body of the despatch, after being concealed in this manner, were then arranged in one or over a thousand possible combinations, the particular combination being indicated by a key word, and as each combination had several key words, it was not necessary to use the same one twice in succession. As a feature of the combination blind words were interspersed at regular or varying intervals, which in translation were of course discarded. When finally prepared for transmission the despatch was wholly unintelligible to the transmitting or receiving operator, and no case can be recalled of the enemy having translated a Federal despatch."

The last statement may seem improbable, but it is absolutely true. Copies of cipher messages frequently fell into the hands of the Confederates and some were even published in the newspapers with request for translation, but not one was successfully untangled. On the other hand the cipher schemes of our opponents were by no means sacred. Many times during the war we solved their carefully drawn despatches and made good use of the information acquired.

The reader can readily imagine that the complexity of the cipher made translation difficult and tiresome. It was no child's play to reduce to intelligible English the weird jumble of meaningless words that made up a message. The utmost care was required in the solution of the puzzle and patience was an indispensible virtue. I may say, however, that even more caution was necessary in transforming the original into the ciphergram. Every mistake made by the operator meant an additional and unexpected task for the man at the other end. Consequently, we who were in the service strove for accuracy by application and painstaking.

I recall an occasion when the blunders of a new man (let us be charitable) furnished me an all night job and caused me to indulge in some pale blue remarks about incompetency, stupidity, &c. After the battle of Chattanooga Grant sent Gen. James H. Wilson of Knoxville to report the situation and condition of Burnside's army. Wilson made a diligent investigation as per orders and forwarded his report to Grant in cipher. It filled several sheets of paper and was comprehensive and detailed.

When I began work on the translation it was about 9 o'clock in the evening. As I progressed I began to find puzzling omissions in the text. There were words left out which should have been put in to make sense, and there were exasperating errors in the use of arbitrary words as well. I knew that the General was anxious to get that report, so I kept at it. I finished my labors at 6 o'clock the next morning. There were thirty-seven mistakes in the message, all of which I had to detect and correct; but the finished translation was the same as the original report.[14]

I don't wish to sing my own praises, but I may be pardoned if I quote my friend Bates (the author of "Lincoln in the Telegraph Office") as to my proficiency with the pen and cipher.

"Capt. Samuel H. Beckwith," he says, "Gen. Grant's cipher operator during his four campaigns, was an expert with the pen, as will be seen from an inspection of his work. His cipher book is truly a work of art. It was his habit all through the war to recopy with a pen the contents of each new edition of our cipher book as fast as supplied to him, and his written copy would be so embellished with extraneous matter as to make it not only attractive from a chirographical point of view, but also wholly unintelligible to any one but a shrewd cipher operator. By the use of ink of various colors he combined two or three different codes in one book."[15]

Secrecy was imperative in the use of all ciphers. To allow several persons to possess the key would naturally be fatal to its secrecy, and the department insisted upon confining it to the fewest possible men consistent with effective service. This fact, I may say, was impressed upon my mind with distressing force in 1864, and I have carried the impression with me ever since. Even at the risk of being tiresome I am going to set forth the incident and the correspondence pertaining thereto, partly because they illustrate the statements I have made about the sanctity of the cipher, and partly, too, because they give an insight into the character of two very distinguished personages.

14. Beckwith probably referred to a telegram from Brig. Gen. James H. Wilson to Grant, Dec. 5, 1863, which will be printed in *PUSG*, IX.
15. Although worded slightly differently, the meaning is the same in Bates, 56–58.

On January 1, 1864, the War Department issued to its operatives in the field the following order:

Ordered, that the cipher books issued by the superintendent of military telegraphs be intrusted only to the care of telegraph experts selected for this duty by the superintendent of telegraphs and approved and appointed by the Secretary of War for duty at the respective headquarters of the military departments and to accompany the armies in the field. The ciphers furnished for this purpose are not to be imparted to any one, but will be kept by the operator to whom they are intrusted in strict confidence and he will be held responsible for their privacy and proper use. They will neither be copied nor used by any other person without special permission from the Secretary of War. Generals commanding will report to the War Department any default of duty by the cipher operators, but will not allow any staff officer to interfere with the operators in the discharge of their duties.

By order of the Secretary of War.

Now it happened that two days prior to the issuance of this order, to be exact, on December 30, 1863, Generals Grant and Thomas broke up housekeeping at Chattanooga, the former removing his headquarters back to Nashville, while he, himself, with a portion of his personal staff, prepared to ride the following day to Knoxville, to inspect Burnside's army. I asked the General if he desired me to accompany him.

"No," he replied considerately, "it will be a long, cold ride, which you may well be spared. I don't think that you will be needed."

In this, however, he was mistaken. Upon his arrival in Knoxville he discovered his error. Cipher messages, which the local operators could not translate, awaited his coming. I was the only one who held the key, and I had been left behind.

To render a recurrence of the embarrassing situation impossible, Grant directed me to give to Col. Comstock, a member of his staff, the key to the cipher. This would be a violation of my instructions, as I interpreted them, for such disclosure was expressly forbidden even to a member of the General's staff. I so informed Grant and suggested that I had better telegraph to the War Department for consent, but the suggestion did not meet his approval. Reluctantly I therefore complied with the request and furnished the key to Comstock, informing Col. Stager, my superior, of my action at once.

When Gen. Halleck, the Administration's military adviser at Washington, learned of the transaction, he became very indignant. In his eyes it was, and perhaps rightly when unexplained, a most grievous breach of trust, and my decapitation was promptly decreed, without the opportunity of a hearing. Grant, however, came to my rescue and saved my imperilled head. This is the correspondence:

HEADQUARTERS OF THE ARMY,
WASHINGTON, January 22, 1864.

Major-Gen. Grant, Chattanooga:

I enclose herewith a copy of a note from Col. Stager in regard to his instructions to Mr. Beckwith respecting the new cipher—.

It was known that the contents of telegrams communicated by means of existing ciphers have been made public without authority. As these ciphers have been communicated to a number of persons the Department was unable to discover the delinquent individual. To obviate this difficulty a new and very complicated cipher was prepared for communications between you and the War Department, which by direction of the Secretary of War was to be communicated to only two individuals, one at your headquarters and one with the War Department. It was to be confided to no one else, not even to me or any member of my staff.

Mr. Beckwith, who was sent to your headquarters, was directed by the Secretary of War to communicate this cipher to no one. In obeying Col. Comstock's orders he disobeyed the Secretary and has been dismissed. He should have gone to prison if Col. Comstock had seen fit to put him there. Instead of forcing the cipher from him, in violation of the order of the War Department, Col. Comstock should have reported the facts of the case here for the information of the Secretary of War, who takes the personal supervision and direction of the military telegraph. On account of the cipher having been communicated to Col. Comstock the Secretary has directed another prepared in its place, which is to be communicated to no one, no matter what his rank, without his special authority.

The Secretary does not perceive the necessity of communicating a special cipher, intended only for telegrams for the War Department, to members of your staff any more than to members of my staff or to the staff officers of other generals commanding geographical departments. All your communications with others are conducted through the ordinary cipher.

It was intended that Mr. Beckwith should accompany you wherever you required him, transportation furnished for that purpose. If by any casualty he should be separated from you communications could be kept up by the ordinary cipher till the vacancy could be supplied.

It is to be regretted that Col. Comstock interfered with the orders of the War Department in this case. As stated in former instructions if any telegraphic employee should not give satisfaction he should be reported and if there be a pressing necessity he may be suspended. But as the corps of telegraphic operators receive their instructions directly from the Secretary of War these should not be interfered with except under very extraordinary circumstances which should be immediately reported.

Very resp'y, &c.
H. W. HALLECK,
Gen'l in Chief.

To this communication Gen. Grant replied first by telegram, and by the following letter of explanation and defence:

HEADQUARTERS MILITARY DIVISION OF THE MISSISSIPPI.

NASHVILLE, Tenn., Feb. 4. 1864.

Major-Gen. H. W. Halleck, General in Chief, Washington, D. C.:

Your letter of the 22d enclosing copy of Col. Stager's of the 21st to you is received.

I will state that Beckwith is one of the best of men. He is competent and industrious. In the matter for which he has been discharged he only obeyed my orders and could not have done otherwise and remain.

On the occasion of going to Knoxville I received Washington despatches which I could not read until my return to this place. To remedy this for the future I directed Col. Comstock to acquaint himself with this cipher. Beckwith desired to telegraph Col. Stager on the subject before complying with my direction. Not knowing of any order defining who and who alone could be intrusted with the Washington cipher, I then ordered Beckwith to give it to Col. Comstock and to inform Col. Stager of the fact that he had done so.

I had no thought in this matter of violating any order or even wish of the Secretary of War. I could see no reason why I was not cabable of selecting a proper person to intrust with this secret, as Col. Stager in fact thought nothing further of the matter than that Col. Stager had his operators under such discipline that they were afraid to obey orders from any one but himself without knowing first his pleasure.

Beckwith has been dismissed for obeying my order. His position is important to him and a better man cannot be selected for it. I respectfully ask that Beckwith be restored. It is not necessary for me to state that I am no stickler for form, but will obey any order or wish from any superior, no matter how conveyed, if I know or only think it came from them. In this instance I supposed Col. Stager was acting for himself and without the knowledge of any one else. I am, General, very respectfully, your obdt. servant,

U. S. GRANT, Maj.-Gen.

I assume that the incident closed with the receipt of Gen. Grant's letter; at any rate I retained my place without further molestation. Of course I was in no way to blame for my violation of orders, for I acted only under the positive command of Grant, but I assure you that for some time I was in grave doubts whether I should retain or lose my position.[16]

A new cipher was immediately devised; for the disclosure of the key to a third person, even though he was a trusted Federal officer, rendered that precaution, so thought the officials in charge, necessary. Needless for me to say the secret remained close locked in my possession, and henceforth the General always took me with him on his travels. One experience of that kind was sufficient for both of us.

That I had in no way lost the absolute confidence and good will of my employer was soon demonstrated to my complete satisfaction. When Grant was promoted to the Lieutenant-Generalship of the army he had to revise somewhat his list of staff and attendants. I was among the very first who were chosen. And he made the announcement of my selection publicly in the office

---

16. Additional correspondence on this matter will be printed in *PUSG*, X.

of the Assistant Adjutant-General in the presence of several officers.

"You have had one tilt with those Washington fellows," he said with a smile, "I reckon you're not afraid of them now. I'll take you with me."

I tried to express my thanks to him for the honor conferred upon me, but he purposely closed the door upon my acknowledgment.

III. Grant, the Soldier.

My appointment of cipher operator to Gen. Grant, as I have stated, established a very close and necessary relationship between him and myself. Of course it was a business relationship, he being my employer and I the subordinate, but constant intimacy engenders friendship and familiarity oftentimes, and I am certain this was the case with the Union commander and his humble servant.

When a message was received, if in cipher, as all messages of any importance were, it was brought to me for translation, and I promptly set to work to make legible the curious confusion of words. It was a task that allowed no procrastination; the fate of the army or of the nation might be involved in the cryptic communication, and expedition upon my part was naturally imperative. The translation completed, I usually carried the despatch myself to the General and waited for his reply, if one was required, which as a rule was immediately forthcoming, for he seldom deliberated long over his responses.

Sometimes he would send his messages to me by orderly; but frequently when one was of considerable importance, he would come himself to my tent or cabin and deliver it to me in person. I remember one or two occasions when he stood patiently and curiously by my side while I transformed his words into the impenetrable puzzle of the cipher. He would appear at all hours of the night regardless of the time, and after I became used to his habits I was not at all startled to see him up and abroad long after midnight. I had read a great deal of Napoleon Bonaparte, how he rarely allowed himself over four or five hours for sleep and how oftentimes he would throw himself upon the ground and command himself to slumber. I don't believe that Grant had any such mastery as that over his mind and body; but I do know that he was distressingly reluctant to waste any time in bed when there was work to do. As for myself, I had to regulate my habits largely by his own and consequently developed into a first class night owl.

The curious thing about the General was that he was just as light an eater as he was a sleeper. His mess table was always frugal and he didn't seem to care for luxuries of any kind; by luxuries I mean desserts, sweetmeats, etc. He had an especial liking for raw oysters, and when these bivalves were in season and could be procured he wanted them before him several times a week. He often made a meal of oysters alone.

It is historical that Grant was an inveterate smoker; but he was not a slave of the weed when I knew him. Sherman and Meade were the champion tobacco consumers of the army; they were veritable chimneys. It is true Grant had the habit fairly well matured, but if reports are trustworthy it must have grown upon him considerably in later years. He sometimes smoked a pipe, a meerschaum usually, a briar occasionally, and sometimes a cigar, and he demanded a reasonably good one too. On starting out in the morning for a tour of inspection or whatever the mission he received from his body servant, a negro named Bill,[17] his cigar case wellstocked, and what he didn't give away during the day to his officers he consumed himself. Being generous with his donations, however, his consumption was not notably abnormal by any means.

This fellow Bill, I may add, understood his master, I believe, better than any one else, not even excepting Rawlins. He seemed to comprehend instinctively all his likes and dislikes. Grant had brought the boy from Cairo and had taken a genuine fancy to him. After his elevation to the Presidency he placed the faithful negro in the Treasury Department as a messenger.

Popularity is something which an officer may or may not enjoy, its enjoyment depending, of course, upon both officer and men. I believe it is true that he who strives to be popular oftentimes loses the sincere esteem of his better fellows. There were some Generals in the army, like Hancock, Ransom, Logan and McPherson, who were idolized by their troops, not because they aspired to popularity, but because of their magnetic soldierly bearing and unassumed democracy of leadership. There were others who, by virtue of weaknesses of character or unfortunate personality, commanded no genuine regard on the part of their following, and hence received only half hearted support. The boys who wore the Federal blue in the sixties were discerning critics; they could readily detect sham and incompetency; and these defects once detected in a leader his period of usefulness was abbreviated.

Gen. Grant was not, perhaps, what might be called a popular hero among his men, and I am certain that he did not aspire to the role. His personal charms were unattractive; his physique was rather squat and unimposing; there was very little of that dashing cavalierism about him that distinguished such commanders as Sheridan and Custer and Hancock and Hooker; but his quiet and thorough efficiency, his self-reliant determination were recognized and felt and secured for him respect and confidence, which are far better than mere popularity. We all liked him, no matter what our station, because he was first of all a soldier; and he was also just and modest and ultimately, so we who knew him best believed, invincible.

Among the many letters and copies of letters that fill my scrap book is the following, which speaks for itself:

17. For William Barnes, a Negro servant who joined Grant during the Vicksburg campaign, see Jesse R. Grant, *In the Days of My Father General Grant* (New York, 1925), 210–11.

HEADQUARTERS DEPARTMENT OF THE TENNESSEE.
VICKSBURG, Miss., 17 August, 1863.

Major-Gen. J. B. MacPherson,[18] Commanding 17th Army Corps:

GENERAL—May I beg the honor of requesting you in behalf of the operators in the field to present the accompanying pair of Major-General's shoulder straps to Major-General U. S. Grant, as a token of respect and esteem.

Should you deem it proper to present them this evening, I beg you will communicate to the General the sincere gratitude which we entertain toward him for the many kindnesses extended to us.

I am, General, with profound respect, &c.,

S. H. BECKWITH,
Operator Gen. Grant's Hdqrs.

Those shoulder straps I had been commissioned by the boys to secure for the General, and each of us had contributed his mite with a right good will. I recall now that I made my purchase in Memphis, and that the donors were well satisfied with my selection. Of course, but a small amount of money was involved in the transaction, but behind it was the real regard of the men for their employer and friend. And after all it isn't the value of the gift in dollars and cents that fixes its true worth, but the spirit that prompts the giving. Judged by this standard that little present was mighty precious.

The obliging MacPherson cheerfully acceded to our request as set forth in my letter, and with a few appropriate words he presented the straps to Grant at the designated time. The response? Well, it was very brief verbally. I don't recall just what it was he said, but we knew that the silent soldier did not underestimate the true worth of our unpretentious gift.

It is an old saying that familiarity breeds contempt. I believe it is also true that the best test of character is the opinion held of him by those who serve him, at least by those who live "with" the man. And it is the exception that proves the rule. We who served Gen. Grant as operators, several of us at any rate, saw much of him, but as the months went by our respect for him strengthened and our regard for him deepened. As for myself—well, I am an old man now and I love him well. The really great never die.

Every man, no matter how serious minded and reserved in manner he may be, has within him somewhere a vein of humor that occasionally manifests itself. Grant, the soldier, was not much given to jesting, in fact he and Lincoln were of wholly different constitution, so far as story telling and joviality were concerned. The former rarely indulged in hearty laughter and his conversation was confined largely to business matters. And yet he had a dry way of saying things that oftentimes brought smiles to the faces of his auditors and indicated that he was not wholly lacking in that physiological curiosity, a funny bone.

18. Maj. Gen. James B. McPherson.

One day when he was in the West and before he became nationally famous, a visitor called on him to inquire concerning the whereabouts of a certain McPherson, who was supposed to belong to Grant's command.

"Have you a McPherson among your men?" the stranger asked.

"Yes, ten McPhersons," replied Grant.

"I mean a certain Sandy McPherson."

"They're all Sandy McPhersons."

"I mean the redheaded one."

"They're all redheaded."

"Humph. But this McPherson has got the itch."

"So have all the McPhersons here," answered Grant.

The visitor passed on to seek information concerning his McPherson elsewhere.

During the Wilderness campaign Rawlins one afternoon was bombarding the inoffensive air with a rich assortment of cuss words. Something had aroused his dander, as the saying goes, and he was exhausting his ingenuity in devising satisfying epithets. Gen. Grant listened for a little while with a deprecating smile on his face and then turning to a bystander, Congressman Washburne, I think it was, he said:

"Do you know why I keep that fellow with me? Well, I keep him to do the cussing for my entire staff, and he makes good, too."

Perhaps a man never lived, with possibly the exception of Job, who had more provocation to resort to profanity than Grant himself. The blunders of his subordinates, the trying situations in which he continually found himself, the thousand and one things that happened to disturb his peace of mind—all these were enough to provoke a preacher to unscriptural wrath; but it was very seldom, indeed, that the General indulged in language that would offend sensitive ears.

The nearest, I believe, that he came to profane remarks was upon an occasion when our train stopped for a few minutes at a rural station in Ohio in 1863. Grant was standing upon the car platform when a rawboned, husky countryman sprang upon the steps and shoving the General to one side, peered into the car. He was, of course, looking for Grant. Catching sight of Ely S. Parker, his military secretary and a full blooded Indian, and mistaking him for the object of his quest because of the brass buttons, he bawled to a gaping companion:

"Hey, Jim, come here; there he is; see that fellow with the buttons; that's him. Gosh, but the old cuss is tanned up."

Grant didn't censure the awkward yokel for his rudeness, but I am reasonably certain that he was sorely tempted to chastise him for his lack of gentleness. As the train pulled out the plainly dressed soldier returned to his seat and surveying Parker for a moment congratulated him upon his distinguished appearance.

I have met many famous men in my lifetime, both in the field and camp and in the byways of peace. Very few of them were of purer morals than was Gen. Grant. His conversation was clean; he had an aversion to obscenity of all kinds. I never heard him tell a salacious story and I know that he disliked to hear one told.

I have sometimes heard it said that the Union commander was a cold and heartless man, a general who won his battles by the sacrifice of thousands of his soldiers, unmoved by the slaughter. And these wise critics point to the Wilderness campaign particularly in confirmation of their argument.

Now I claim that my intimate association with Grant all during that eventful year of 1864 gives me some authority to speak and to speak intelligently upon the subject, and I know whereof I write. I can bear positive witness that the aspersions cast upon his humanity and magnanimity are grossly unjust. Consider the condition of affairs a moment. There was only one way to conquer the forces of the Confederacy and that was the way adopted by Gen. Grant, to keep pounding away at them until their inferior resources were exhausted. It must be remembered that Lee was fighting now upon the defensive, that the problem confronting the Federal leader was not how to protect the North from invasion but how to capture Richmond and destroy the enemy.

Other commanders had labored too persistently under the idea that the object of the war was to prevent the Southern armies from seizing Washington. Lincoln, Stanton and Grant always insisted that the one object of the war was the downfall of the Confederate capital and the surrender of those in arms against the flag. Every life lost in the accomplishment of this result was a regrettable but necessary incident in the attainment of the end. There was terrible slaughter in the spring of 1864, but what master genius of history could have met Robert E. Lee on his own territory, accomplished as much as did Grant in so brief a time and lessened that slaughter by a man?

Ulysses S. Grant was not a Bonaparte; he was a great soldier who planned his campaigns and doggedly carried out his plans like a soldier, conserving so far as possible the lives of his men. It is absolutely untrue that he valued human life lightly and viewed the loss of his troops with callous equanimity. The fearful casualties of the Wilderness, of bloody Spottsylvania, of Cold Harbor weighed upon this burdened man heavily. He was noticeably depressed and unusually reticent. I believed then and I am convinced now that he suffered keenly in his quiet and undemonstrative way at the expenditure of patriot blood.

I remember an instance when the human side of Grant was graphically revealed to me. In October of 1864 Gen. Thomas E. G. Ransom, formerly of the old Eleventh Illinois, died at a farm house while being borne to Rome, Ga., by litter for treatment. This young officer had served under Gen. Grant in his campaigns in the West and had won his superior's sincere admiration by his chivalrous conduct upon the battlefield. There was no better or braver soldier in the army than Ransom. Sherman's announcement of his death, in cipher, reached City Point, Va., Grant's headquarters in the operations before Petersburg, late at night. I made a hurried translation of the message, and knowing the regard he entertained for the dead leader, I went to his tent and found the General alone, sitting at a table studying a field map.

I announced my presence by laying my hand lightly upon his shoulder, while with the other I handed him the despatch. He read it in silence. I saw that he was struggling with his emotions, for his lips twitched and his eyes closed as if he were in pain. Then, and apparently with an effort, he regained his composure, while a telltale tear stole down his bronzed cheek. Quickly he drew out a sheet of paper from his desk and wrote to Stanton, requesting the Secretary to make Ransom a Major-General, to date from the day of his death, and to send the commission to the dead soldier's mother. Not a word had been spoken by either of us, and without lifting his head he handed the telegram to me. I quietly left the tent and within fifteen minutes had sent the generous message to Washington.[19]

One of Grant's marked characteristics, to which reference has been made, was his reticence; he was one of the most reserved men I have ever known. The faculty of restraint both in speech and in expression of the feelings was pronounced; and this faculty frequently induced the impression among those who met him that he was cold and untutored in the ways of the sociable world. I don't believe that this manner was in any degree assumed; he couldn't help it any more than Lincoln could forego his humor or his tenderness of heart. Many a time did the General order me to accompany him upon his rides (he and I alone); for I am proud to say that he seemed to find in me an agreeable comrade; and side by side we would cover mile after mile without the interchange of a word, he evidently pondering the varied problems of the campaign, while I, accustomed to his habits, preserved a sympathetic silence.

Grant was a first class horseman, in fact one of the most adept in the army. He had acquired a thorough mastery of the steed at West Point, where his proficiency in handling his mount won for him the commendation of cadets and faculty alike. And that mastery was recognized now by officers and privates. His was not what would be called an imposing figure, but he rode with such careless ease that he seemed very much at home in the saddle. When the weather was mild he generally wore while riding a regulation blue blouse

19. Brig. Gen. Thomas E. G. Ransom died on Oct. 29, 1864. On Nov. 6, Grant wrote to Secretary of War Edwin M. Stanton requesting an appointment of brevet maj. gen. for Ransom. U.S. War Department, *The War of the Rebellion: A Compilation of the Official Records of the Union and Confederate Armies* (Washington, 1880–1901), I, xxxix, part 3, 657. The appointment was made as of Sept. 1.

without the coat. He seldom carried a sword and manifestly had no liking for the trappings and show of rank.

An occasional historian has dwelt at some length upon the mounts that Grant had during the war. Usually three are mentioned—Little Jeff, Egypt and Cincinnati. There was a fourth, Old Jack, that the General rode at Forts Henry and Donelson and during the Holly Springs campaign, a clay bank stallion of fighting mettle highly prized by his master.

IV. Stanton.

Nothing short of a question of vital importance could have prompted Secretary Stanton's order to Gen. Grant at Vicksburg appointing Indianapolis as the meeting place for a personal conference to be held on Sunday, October 18, 1863. In obedience to instructions Grant and his entire staff, headquarters, camp and garrison outfit boarded a special train for the Indiana city.

As we drew into the station at Indianapolis at noon on the appointed day a train from the East came in and pulled up alongside. A plainly dressed civilian attended by a single staff officer descended from a coach and approached our car. They were Stanton and Col. Stager, chief of military telegraphs. Their entire baggage consisted of a basket of grapes, part of the contents of which they had consumed.

It was the first time that I had seen the War Secretary and I was considerably impressed by his distinguished appearance.

I made a hurried inventory of the statesman in a few seconds, for he came immediately to our train and took a seat beside Gen. Grant, who had gone to the door to meet him. All the afternoon these two men remained in close conference, unmindful of all else save only the grave questions they were debating. Early in the evening we reached Louisville, Ky. Grant and Stanton hurried to the Galt House, where, heedless of the supper hour, they continued their consultation until midnight.

I had of course put up at the same hotel and was lingering about the lobby awaiting developments. Shortly after 12 o'clock Stanton approached me with energetic step, and addressing me by name, much to my astonishment, handed me two papers, at the same time giving me explicit oral instructions as to their disposition. I asked the Secretary if he would kindly read the papers to me and he readily complied. One was an order removing Gen. Rosecrans from the command of the Army of the Cumberland, the other was the appointment to the command of Gen. George H. Thomas. I at once hastened to the Western Union office and had the despatches transmitted in cipher.

The results of that conference were, in brief, these: Grant was to command a military division of three departments—Tennessee, Cumberland and Ohio—and he was to remain with the army to direct its movements and operations. Thomas was to supersede Rosecrans in the command of the Army of the Cumberland.

While I am upon the subject of Stanton I may as well devote a few lines to other occasions when I met the Secretary, not that there is any particular historical significance attached to the meetings, but because anecdotes of this nature, and there has been a wealth of them, reveal the character of the man far better than mere description.

Some months after my first interview with him I received a telegram which called for immediate action. I briefed out the matter on a sheet of paper and hurried to the War Department. Stanton's private office was on the second floor, northeast corner of the building, where none but official callers were admitted during business hours. Across the corridor was a public chamber, where asembled all others who wished audience with him. As soon as I entered the corridor I encountered the Secretary's son, to whom I handed a note requesting him to ask his father to read it at once. In a few minutes I was summoned to the private room. Stanton was standing near the door, and seeing my embarrassment (for there was something about him that rather confused me), he motioned me to a desk near by, at the same time very considerately laying before me paper and pen.

"Write what you wish and I will sign it," he said.

This bit of strategy dispelled my nervousness. I handed him back the pen, and apologizing for my weakness, stated my errand. He at once seated himself at the desk and in a brief time handed me two orders, the one that I sought, the other a demand for strict enforcement. In his brusque and business manner he said:

"Take this to the operating room of the Western Union; listen, and be sure it is transmitted immediately and accurately."

Both commands were obeyed. The second order, which illustrates Stanton's attention to detail, was direction to the manager of the telegraph office to send a trustworthy operator to identify and deliver, a precaution that demanded responsibility of prompt delivery.

In the winter of 1864-5 Secretary Stanton visited Admiral Porter, who was then on board the Malvern anchored in the stream at City Point. While the two were at dinner an important cipher message came from Washington for the Cabinet official. I did not send an orderly to deliver it, as I might have done; but wishing to assure myself of its speedy and safe carriage I jumped myself aboard the first tug that steamed out and went to the flagship. A colored servant carried my sealed package within and almost immediately the War Secretary in evening dress left the banquet table and with the papers in his hand came to me. His face expressed the cordiality of his feelings as he said:

"Mr. Beckwith, I wish to thank you personally for the pains you have taken to honor me by this visit."

Candidly, I was quite surprised at his unusual benevolence.

I remember well going one day to the War Office on a matter of no great moment, taking my seat in the southwest corner of the room. There was the usual crowd of petitioners assembled, each one with some favor to ask or complaint to register. As my business was not pressing I determined to await my turn and observe Stanton's reception of visitors. As one after another presented his or her request, I studied the Secretary's face. It was like adamant. If he felt any emotion engendered by appeal or criticism his features did not reveal it. I suppose that he had become so accustomed and inured to this bombardment that he was almost immune to its attack.

Now and then he turned to Gen. Hardee[20] who was standing at his right and gave him some quick, short order in a low voice. Once he indicated to me that I could have precedence if I so desired it, but I shook my head and awaited my turn. A little woman in widow's weeds was ahead of me and I let her have her inning with the Secretary. I could overhear the conversation. She wanted reinstatement to a clerkship from which she had been ousted for some reason or other, and she told a very human and touching little story. But I was unable to discover in Stanton's face any trace of sympathy or response. He listened attentively, it is true, but whether she made any impression upon him was more than I could tell. As she turned away I stepped forward, and at once the sphinx-like countenance relaxed into smiles, as he related to Hardee the circumstances of the lady's dismissal. The story told, he turned to me, the same brusque and serious official, and signed the order that I held in my hand.

Was he incapable of the tenderer emotions? I am certain that he was a very human man in spite of his rough and determined exterior. He was the engineer in charge of the complex machinery of a department that was of tremendous moment and mighty responsibility. If he lacked the vibrant heart of Lincoln, we must remember that he was cast of sterner mould; that his dominant will and inflexible patriotism were invaluable assets to the Government when such qualities were most needed. There have been greater statesmen than Stanton; but no nation in its hour of peril ever had a more zealous and loyal son.

V. Chattanooga.

Once more let me say that it is not my purpose, in these brief memoirs, to describe campaigns and battles which already have been fully described by far more competent historians. I don't presume to any superior knowledge of history; and inasmuch as they whose genius directed the various combats have written largely of them it would be idle for me to attempt any addition

20. Brig. Gen. James A. Hardie.

thereto. I wish, however, to devote just a little space to "Chattanooga"; not to the fight itself, but to some of the incidents that fell under my personal observation and with which the reader is not perhaps familiar. I trust at least that it will not be mere repetition.

As a result of the conference before set forth Gen. Grant was now in command of the military division of the Mississippi and under orders to proceed immediately to the front. The front was at Chattanooga, where lay the Army of the Cumberland under Thomas in a state of siege, with the enemy's lines stretching from the Tennessee River on the east, along Missionary Ridge, across the Chattanooga Valley to Lookout Mountain.

On the morning of October 21, 1863, Gen. Grant, accompanied by a few of his staff officers and myself, took a train at Nashville for the beleaguered town. There was no question that the Federal forces were in a serious predicament, and the problem that confronted the Union commander was how to extricate them successfully from this menacing situation. Fortunately for the troops and country a man had been chosen who was equal to the emergency.

We reached Stevenson, Ala., in the early evening. Gen. Rosecrans and Capt. Van Duzer, the chief of the military telegraphs of the Army of the Cumberland, were in the village and met us at the station. I wasn't immensely impressed with the beauty of the former, I am willing to confess. He had a very large face and a prominent nose that suggested Jewish extraction and he was considerably overweight for a fighter, so I thought at the time. The soldiers called him Old Rosy and the name seemed appropriate. He went at once to Grant's car and remained in consultation with the General for ten or fifteen minutes. Van Duzer, in the meantime, came over to me and requested that I intercede with my chief that he might permit him a few moments conversation.

It seems that some time prior to this, at Holly Springs in 1862, Van Duzer, who was in the employ of the War Department, had refused to obey an order given him by Grant, and as a result the best of feeling had not existed since then between them.[21] The young officer, now that Rosecrans was relieved, was very fearful lest he too must walk the plank and was consequently desirous of petitioning Gen. Grant for his retention.

As soon as Rosecrans left the car I went in and informed Grant of Van Duzer's request, explaining the situation in a few words.

"Let him come in," said he. "I don't want to open old sores. What's past is past. All I ask is that he do his work and obey orders."

I conveyed this message to the anxious Captain, who grasped my hand gratefully. With a smile of relief he entered the car. The interview lasted about thirty seconds, but that was long enough. Van Duzer kept his job and a year

21. See *PUSG*, VI, 377-85.

later distinguished himself by wiring to anxious Washington the first news of the battle of Nashville and the splendid victory of Thomas.

From Stevenson we continued our journey to Bridgeport, where we spent the night. The next day, immediately after breakfast, we took to the saddle, Gen. O. O. Howard, who was stationed near the village, riding with us as far as Anderson.

The memory of that ride yet lingers with me and it is a rather painful recollection at that. For several days past heavy rains had fallen and the roads were almost impassable from the mud, which in many places came well up to our boots. Our horses were frequently to their knees in the soft mire, and in some spots where the mountain streams, swollen to little torrents, had washed away the earth, we had to dismount and pick our way to more stable ground. All this must have been exquisite torture to Grant, who was suffering from an injury received in the late summer in New Orleans by the falling of his horse. The jarring jolts of the trip left me with tender memories for several days and I presume that the General was more severely afflicted. But he bore the rigors of the way with Indian stoicism and no complaint escaped his lips.

It was very manifest that we were in the midst of an arena of serious warfare. The roads over which we travelled were cluttered with broken down wagons and the carcasses of mules and horses that the grim hand of starvation and disease had laid low. There must have been thousands of these poor beasts scattered along the way and they presented mute and convincing evidence of the dire peril that clutched at the throat of the Union army. Surely the men themselves must be in sore straits, and my heart beat in keen sympathy for the boys in blue who were experiencing the bitter reality of implacable strife.

When we reached Anderson, we halted again for the night. It was raining, a steady, dreary autumn downpour, and although we were covered with oilcloth from chin to knee, we were all drenched to the skin. It was certainly a most cheerless prospect. I was completely tired out and chilled to the marrow, so I at once hunted up quarters at a private house and lost no time in crawling into bed.

When I awoke in the morning a disagreeable surprise awaited me. I had overslept the hour of departure and Grant and his companions had gone. That was his habit of business as I well knew, but it was the first time that I had been the victim of it. He was like time and tide that wait for no man. We who served him were supposed to be "on the job" at the stroke of the clock; if we failed to respond—well, we had to do as I did, that's all.

I snatched a hasty breakfast and started in pursuit of the vigilant party; but as luck would have it, I took the wrong road and lost my bearings. Instead of going through Anderson's Pass, the route taken by the others, I headed for the summit of Waldron's Ridge, a blunder which cost me much time and distance. All day long I climbed the muddy roadway, cursing my inexcusable tardiness, and night overtook me as I reached the crest. You may imagine my condition. I was as wet as the proverbial drowned rat, absolutely exhausted and famished from my ten hours fast. Fortunately I found a good Samaritan, a farmer whose name I shall carve high on memory's tablet among the benefactors of mankind, who took me in and gave me shelter and food. It was with a feeling of blessed release from torment that I threw myself in my dripping garments before the crackling warmth of the fire to sleep till dawn.

It was well along in the afternoon when I rode into Chattanooga. I hunted up Rawlins, Grant's chief of staff, and reported my safe arrival. He asked me if I had dined and I told him I had eaten a can of sardines which I had begged from a sutler's wagon on the road and nothing else since morning.

"Well," he commented in characteristic manner, "you are damned lucky to have got that; it's more than we've had here."

That was slight distortion of the truth, of course; but I found that his statement was not wholly misrepresentative of the actual conditions. For days our troops had been subsisting upon half rations of hard bread and a few ounces of tough, almost inedible beef that would have better served for boot soles than for meat. The rank of the soldier didn't seem to make any difference either; Thomas himself was a willing victim of the poverty of [the] sources. The gaunt spectre of hunger was stalking through the camp, but under the indomitable leadership of their brave commanders, our boys were holding resolutely against discouragement with strong hearts and true Northern courage. It was admirable the way they accepted their hard lot and cheerfully endured the rigors of their privations.

Bright and early on the morning after his arrival, so I learned that evening, Grant had begun to reconnoitre the Confederate lines, so anxious was he to ascertain the precise situation and strength of the opposing forces and the difficulty of the problem that confronted him. On nearing the Chickamauga Creek bridge, he had been recognized by the men, who gave him an enthusiastic greeting, evidently seeing in his advent the promise of speedy and longed for relief. The Union officer on duty promptly ordered out the picket; but the General, always disliking unnecessary personal honors, restrained him from the customary formality. A little spontaneous enthusiasm on the part of his troops was much more satisfying to him, and his face lighted up with an expression of pleasure when they insisted, nevertheless, on showing their feelings in a rousing cheer.

The Confederate officer on the opposite bank of the stream, however, was not amenable to orders. Observing the Federal commander, he sang out in a loud voice:

"Turn out the guard; the commanding General!"

Whereupon our friends, the "Johnnies," turned out and toed the mark at present arms, a tribute which the Northern leader courteously acknowledged with a salute.

What happened during the ensuing month what preparations were made, what activity displayed, is of course history. Grant was the soul of soldierly intrepidity. I can bear witness that his presence did more to keep glowing the fires of confidence than anything else. He impressed even me, who had seen so much of him, with his indefatigable industry. If the far famed Corsican warrior had "anything on him" for diligence and watchfulness I mistake my knowledge of both men; and I am fairly conversant with the achievements of the illustrious Frenchman. Science teaches us that food is essential to labor. Well, surely, much food is not necessary for much labor, for Grant's appetite would have discouraged an average cook. I'll wager that I ate more in one meal than he did in three, and I am not a gormand by any means. He was equally sparing with sleep, and how he maintained his maximum of power on a minimum of fuel is beyond my understanding. I naturally seldom indulged myself to excess in the nectar of Morpheus, but as I have already indicated I kept my end well up at the mess tent and hence got along nicely. The General—but what is the use of explaining; he can't be judged by the average standard, that's all.

I don't wish to impute to Grant all credit for the splendid successes in and about Chattanooga, much as I am devoted to him and to his memory. A commander never had more zealous men to work with or better officers to carry out his plans. There were with us there some of the war's best Generals, whose ability and heroism had been tested and found sterling. Sherman, Osterhaus and Sheridan were a triumvirate that was most formidable. And then, too, there was Thomas, who in himself was a host.

Gen. George H. Thomas, who had been placed in charge of the Army of the Cumberland, was a Virginian by birth and a credit to that State that has given to the nation so many useful and distinguished sons. He was a natural fighter and throughout his many campaigns had never learned the definition of the word surrender. I saw a great deal of him in this campaign and became one of his many warm admirers. There were some striking similarities and a few dissimilarities between him and Grant. He was not a large man, but he was the picture of soldierly dignity and circumspection. His strong bearded face revealed in its every feature decision and purpose. He was never talkative, but when he did speak he always said something worth the hearing. On the field he saw everything that went on and seemed to grasp intuitively a situation at a glance.

Unlike his superior, however, he was not a quick worker. He planned carefully and worked cautiously; at times his deliberation appeared censurable, but when he was ready to strike he struck home with a blow that carried annihilation and dismay to the enemy. Fame has immortalized him as the "Rock of Chickamauga" and the "Sledge of Nashville." She might well have bestowed some verbal decoration upon him for his services at Chattanooga. His soldiers affectionately dubbed him Pap Thomas, and they trusted his leadership with an almost blind devotion. He never lost their trust.

At the battle of Lookout Mountain I saw these two peerless soldiers when the crisis proves the man and the picture is still before me. With their staffs they had taken their posts at Fort Negley, a bombproof structure situated at the base of the hill. I stood throughout the engagement almost at Grant's elbow and was a most interested observer of the progress of the battle and of the men who directed it. Both officers were garbed with the utmost simplicity. Gen. Grant wore his plain service coat and a slouch hat pulled down over his eyes. His trousers were tucked into his boots and he wore neither sword nor gloves. Thomas was perhaps even more inconspicuous; an oilcloth cloak covered him from chin to boot and the only thing that indicated his rank was his hat with its little acorn tipped bullion cord about it. One might have mistaken him for a civilian spectator of events.

The struggle up Lookout's rugged slope is undoubtedly one of the most familiar of the war to present generations on account of its spectacular features. As the "Battle above the Clouds" it has been celebrated in song and story, and yet in reality the battle in the fog would describe it better. The mountain doesn't reach the required altitude of 2,000 feet and hence, under normal conditions, falls a trifle short of cloudland. The day on which the engagement was staged, however, was certainly extremely foggy and therefore by poetic license I presume the characterization of the school books is proper. One thing is beyond dispute, and that is that a most thrilling and picturesque charge was spoiled, from a spectator's viewpoint, by the obscuring curtain that was drawn over the arena. Occasionally it would part and for a moment we could glimpse the colors of Osterhaus's advancing troops; then it would roll together and only the crash of artillery would evidence the progress of the fight.

Despite the fact that the contest was one of grave moment, both Generals were remarkably cool and undisturbed. I didn't hear much conversation between them, and I believe that you would have a vain search to find two big men who could do more and say less than Grant and Thomas. Once in a while the former would draw a cigar from his case and puff away at it complacently while he peered through the veil before him and listened to the welcome sound of battle. The latter never used tobacco, at least I never saw him indulge in the habit in any form, and I venture to assert that his iron nerves needed no narcotic in times of stress and storm. I wondered at the seeming indifference, or shall I say assurance, of these commanders in whose hands was the success or failure of the combat, but I know that beneath the placid exterior were minds vigilant and masterful.

That Grant had a most encouraging confidence in his officers who were executing the movements about Chattanooga was demonstrated repeatedly during the preliminary operations and the two days struggle itself. In Sherman he always reposed implicit faith. In Sheridan he had an almost equal trust. I remember an illustration of this latter statement on the afternoon of the second day. It will be recalled that Gen. Sheridan was ordered to take the first line of rifle pits on the slope of Missionary Ridge and, this accomplished, to halt and reform. Carried away apparently by the enthusiasm of the charge, the Union troops, driving the enemy from their entrenchments followed them in lusty pursuit up the hill, regardless of orders.

Grant had been watching the movement with quiet eagerness. When our boys swept beyond the position that had been fixed for their reforming a murmur of surprise arose from the little party of staff officers about me. A palpable violation of instructions! A miscarriage of plans! What was Sheridan thinking of! A young lieutenant at my side hastily approached the General and exclaimed in great perturbation:

"Why, General, they are not even stopping to reform."

Without removing his earnest gaze from the stirring scene, without even a twitch of a muscle, Grant replied in his matter of fact way:

"Let 'em go, Sheridan will come out all right."

When one considers that the onward rush of the Union forces was an open disregard of plans; was in fact a possibly dangerous disorganization of formation that might invite defeat, one must appreciate the sincere respect that the Federal leader entertained for his lion hearted commander.

I have read many descriptions of that spectacular ascent, but none of them adequately portrays the real grandeur of the scene. Pen and brush are unequal to the task. It must have been seen and heard in all its wondrous action and colors and thunders of sound to be fully realized. Never did battle have a more magnificent setting—the calm and clear November day, the keen tang of the early winter air, off to the right Lookout Mountain, with its scarred face; before us the immense acclivity of Missionary Ridge, crowded with Confederate batteries and alive with waving battleflags—surely an arena worthy of the bravest struggle. And it was a charge that stirred the heart and thrilled the soul. I am glad that it was my lot to witness it, and it is a safe prediction that never again will this progressive, peace loving and powerful nation see its like. It was the brightest page of Grant's military history.

VI. Petersburg.

Grant's scheme for ending the war, as all students of history know, was to impoverish the Confederate forces by cutting off their lines of supply, while he kept up a persistent and wearing offence against their inferior numbers. In June of 1864 he designed to get south of Richmond, destroy the Virginia Central Railroad and capture Petersburg. If he succeeded in this plan but one line, the Richmond and Danville, would remain open. This he would close as soon as possible and the Southern capital must fall.

Early in the morning of the 17th of June, by a very skilful movement, the entire Federal army passed south of the James River. Grant sent by orderly a cipher despatch to me for transmission to President Lincoln, announcing his progress; and the Executive immensely gratified at the celerity of his trusted General, responded in those characteristic words:

"I have just received your despatch of 1 P. M. yesterday. I begin to see it. You will succeed. God bless you all."

The seizure of Petersburg, the primary object of the campaign, was no child's play. It was, in fact, the city I mean, the gateway, to Richmond, lying but twenty-two miles to the south. Its capture meant the inevitable downfall of the capital. But it was an enterprise fraught with tremendous difficulties. The defences began far beyond Grant's extreme left and extended around to the Appomattox River. Thence they ran northward so as to protect the Richmond and Petersburg line from molestation. The fortifications immediately before Petersburg, thrown up under the watchful eyes of trained engineers, were of the most formidable kind, and they were defended by disciplined troops. The struggle for supremacy must necessarily be a contest of strategy, of assault and repulse, of toil and hardship; protracted, perhaps, but persistent.

It would be mere repetition of familiar facts for me to describe the operations of our armies about historic Petersburg, and I am not desirous of boring my readers with any such recital. Carrying coals to Newcastle is an occupation that is both laborious and useless. I presume that the little I have to say will seem more or less trite, but inasmuch as it all happened under my very eyes, I may be pardoned for writing about it.

As soon as we were established at City Point, the urgent necessity of the erection of a military telegraph line became manifest to the General. He accordingly directed me to send the following telegram forthwith:

HEADQUARTERS ARMIES OF THE UNITED STATES.
CITY POINT, Va., June 16, 1864.
Mr. R. O'Brien, Chief Operator, Headquarters Department Virginia and North Carolina:

DEAR SIR—General Grant directs that a line be constructed from these headquarters to Gen. Butler's headquarters and office opened here as soon as possible. He also orders the construction of a line from Gen. Meade's headquarters; and as Mr. Caldwell is short of operators, perhaps you have one or two to spare. I think Doren is at work down from Fort Powhatten, but have not heard to-day. Please let me know when you can complete the line to this place and how you are off for operators. Yours, &c.,

S. H. BECKWITH.

These directions were speedily carried out; we were placed in direct communication with the War Department at Washington by way of Fortress Monroe, and a line was run to Meade's headquarters in front of Petersburg and to Butler's at Bermuda Hundred. With commendable expedition a complete system of wires was perfected, uniting the various important posts, depots and entrenchments, and extending as far, in some instances, as the picket. The offices were rude and unpretentious, as might be expected; battery wagons were fitted up in some places to accommodate the apparatus and operator; while in others, tents were used for this service.

It may be assumed that the life of the military telegraphers was one of comparative security; but the assumption would be most incorrect. Plum is authority for the statement that "about one in twelve of the operators engaged in the service were killed, wounded, captured or died in the service from exposure."[22] They were frequently subjected to the fire of the enemy and were obliged oftentimes to resort to bombproof offices for protection against danger. But they stuck to their tasks valiantly and rendered as faithful service to the country as did the soldiers in the field.

Gen. Grant, on leaving headquarters for the field, usually rode either Cincinnati or Little Jeff, the former being his favorite horse. He took me with him on most of these trips and as he was on the go a great deal of the time, inspecting the works and discussing plans with his Generals, we were in the saddle a substantial portion of the campaign. He was not what would be called in the country an early riser. No one who kept the late hours that he did—we seldom retired before midnight—could get up with the sun and preserve his health and strength. He arose when he felt like it, and that was usually somewhere around 7 o'clock, and he made every hour of the working day count. Of course I do not pose as an authority upon the qualifications of a commanding officer; but it seemed to me then that Grant possessed all the requirements, whatever they were. He was active, earnest, persistent and intelligent, and it was not his blame that the siege was long drawn out and disappointing in its many reverses.

The tedium of the daily routine in camp and in the trenches was occasionally broken by incidents that left their impress on all who witnessed them. I will mention only two of the "disasters" that seemed to follow the Federal army for months and unnerve the arm that should have quickly broken the defences of the Confederates.

In the fore part of August a catastrophe, not large perhaps in the number of casualties but very distressing nevertheless, happened at City Point. Losses upon the battlefield are sad enough, but when death comes in the form of sudden calamity to soldiers within the security of their lines it seems especially deplorable.

At the City Point wharf on the morning of the 9th lay an ordnance boat with a supply of shells and ammunition for the troops at the front. There were several of the crew aboard and some soldiers standing on the dock. On the bluff near by a train was about to start out toward Petersburg, and the cars

22. Plum, II, 352.

were filled with boys on their way to the intrenchments. I was sitting in my tent writing a letter and awaiting the orders of the General.

A terrific crash brought me to my feet. From some unaccountable cause the cargo on the ordnance boat exploded, blowing the vessel and wharf to smithereens and hurling shells and timber and shot and fragments of human bodies in all directions. One shell hurtled through my tent and set fire to the covering of my bed scarcely five feet from where I was sitting. Hastily smothering the flames, I rushed out to ascertain the nature of the explosion and the extent of the damage. Soldiers were scurrying this way and that seeking to escape the shower of missiles which was falling about them. I saw several of the officers crouching behind convenient trees. The surface of the water and the ground around me were strewn with debris. Sixty men had been killed outright and over a hundred and thirty wounded.

Grant and the members of his staff escaped unscathed, and several of them assisted in caring for the injured. It was but one link in the chain of misfortune that held fast the Union army in its operations before Petersburg.

I know that the reader is more or less conversant with the facts of the bungling attack that has gone down in history as the mine fiasco. I don't assume, therefore, to write of it as of some unpublished event. But possibly a brief narration of a few of the details may be interesting to those who were not present and who are not diligent students of rebellion battles and sieges.

The Forty-eighth Pennsylvania, a regiment of coal miners, had run a mine under a section of the Confederate fortifications, it being the intention to explode it and thereby effect a breach in the works. Minute instructions had been given for the assault which was to follow the explosion, and it was confidently expected that a way would be broken through which the entering wedge could be thrust.

It had been planned to touch off the mine at about 4 o'clock in the morning of the 30th. Gen. Grant with a few of his staff and myself left City Point by train shortly before daylight to witness the coup de main. We had put our horses on board one of the cars, and after we had travelled by rail as far as we could we mounted and continued our way.

When we got to the scene of action we found that arrangements had somewhat gone amiss. The fuse running to the mine failed to ignite properly and a very tedious and anxious delay ensued while the difficulty was being remedied. I remember that I finally became wearied of waiting, and being sleepy I retired to one of the officers' tents to steal a few moments rest. Grant also, I believe, impatient at the loss of precious time, left the place and was not a spectator of the actual explosion.

Shortly before 5 o'clock the four tons of powder stored beneath the salient were touched off and the muffled boom shook the earth beneath me. I ran from the tent and tried to secure a vantage point from which I could see the result of the mighty upheaval and the assault which I knew would now come.

An immense crater had been torn in the enemy's works and a gateway was opened by which our troops could secure a foothold within.

But the well laid plans and confident expectations were badly shattered. It is a matter of general knowledge how the pitiable incapacity of the officers charged with the execution of those plans brought defeat and humiliation to our troops and chagrin to the entire army. Burnside, who had been intrusted with the enterprise, was unequal to the emergency. He seemed to have paid no attention whatever to the instructions so carefully given and to have left everything to chance.

Gen. J. H. Ledlie had been selected by Burnside, by lot it was reported, to lead the assailing forces. Some time prior to this Ledlie had come to me with a letter of introduction from Major James R. O'Beirne, in which the latter spoke in praise of his ability as a soldier and requested me to use my good offices with Grant to secure for him a command in the army. I learned that he was from Utica, N. Y., and that he was anxious to land a berth in the Army of the Potomac. I took the letter to the General and left it with him. It must have made an impression, for the petition was granted.

The assignment of Ledlie to this important task was a most lamentable blunder. He was, I have no doubt, a fair engineer; but he was a mighty poor commanding officer, being wofully deficient in those soldierly qualities that go to constitute capable leadership.

It had been planned to throw a force into and through the breach to gain a strategic point, Cemetary Hill, overlooking the city. The movement was wretchedly executed. The troops advanced tardily and slowly, and when at length in motion they rushed up to the huge pit only to find it filled with debris. As they stumbled over it and into the crater a merciless fire swept them from left, right and front. Gen. Ledlie, as Grant put it, "had found some safe retreat to get into before they started" (as a matter of fact, a bomb proof), and the men were apparently left to the subordinate officers. They faltered and lost heart. Then as the enemy rallied from the shock and their fire became hotter our boys huddled together in a confused mass, like cattle awaiting the slaughter, company formation gone, black and white mingled—negro troops had been sent in to save the day—a pitiable mob, seeking as best they could escape from death.

Grant, who had returned to the scene, viewed the heartbreaking miscarriage of plans with much concern. He had dismounted from his horse and he now went forward on foot to see at closer range the true state of affairs. He was soon convinced that the much hoped for effort was a stupendous failure. There was only one thing to do, and that was to extricate the men from their perilous position as quickly as possible, a task by no means easy. It was not until noon that they were withdrawn under Meade's orders. It had cost our army 4,000 men in killed and prisoners; and the blame could be rightly imputed not to the framers of the plan, certainly not to the men themselves, but to the inefficiency of those who were charged with the success of the assault, the corps and division commanders.

It was a bitter disappointment to Gen. Grant, who had anticipated excellent results from the operation. All summer long things had been breaking poorly, as the saying is, and this new and considerable disaster must have weighed heavily upon him. So far as I know, however, he did not voice his condemnation publicly or privately, for he seldom gave way to passion; but I know that he was very much disgusted with the whole enterprise. The following Monday—the 30th was Saturday—he delivered to me a despatch for Meade that expressed well his feelings.

(Cipher.)   CITY POINT, Aug. 1, 1864.
Major-Gen. Meade.

Have you any estimate of our losses in the miserable failure of Saturday? I think there will have to be an investigation of the matter. So fair an opportunity will probably never occur again for carrying fortifications. Preparations were good, orders ample, and everything, so far as I could see, subsequent to the explosion of the mine, shows that almost without loss the crest beyond the mine could have been carried. This would have given us Petersburg with all its artillery and a large part of its Garrison beyond doubt.

Intercepted despatch states that the enemy recaptured their line, with Gen. Bartlett & staff, seventy-five commissioned officers and nine hundred rank & file and recaptured five hundred of their men.

U. S. GRANT,
Lt. Gen.[23]

The reader will recall that Meade censured the culpable Burnside in strong language for the "miserable failure" and promptly preferred charges against him. A few days afterward the offending officer was relieved of command. Lincoln some time later ordered a court of inquiry and the General and several of his subordinates were reprimanded for neglect of duty.

VII. The Brighter Side.

The ancient adage that every cloud has its silver lining found realization at City Point in 1864. The monotony of the operations in the field was relieved by many diverting episodes that served to make life endurable and even at times pleasurable. The history of those long months of siege, of toilsome endeavor, of planning, of misfortunes had also its bright pages of happy incidents that cheered the camp at headquarters and the soldiers in the ranks.

Gen. Grant and his staff were not always riding the lines and inspecting the offensive works. There was a substantial part of the real labor performed at

---

23. Beckwith owned the original telegram, which was reproduced in facsimile with his article in the *Sun.*

City Point and there was a great deal of the routine of the campaign quietly and effectively conducted in the tents and cabins that has been unsung.

Perhaps you have wondered what necessitated my remaining on duty until midnight and after. Well, I assure you that it was not any aversion to sleep or a desire to witness the sun rise. We had tasks to discharge and these compelled our persistent attention. Along in the early evening we began to look for reports from our armies operating in other sections of the country. These came of course in cipher and I was the one who had to make them intelligible for the General's perusal.

In the late summer and autumn Sherman was down in Georgia with his "bummers" on the way to the sea. Sheridan was in the Shenandoah Valley; and in the latter part of November and the fore part of December Thomas was preparing to thrash Hood's forces at Nashville. Hence Grant wanted news, and his mind naturally dwelt many times a day upon these sterling commanders and the problems that confronted them. It can be appreciated how trememdous was the responsibility that rested upon his shoulders when one reflects that the direction and control of all the armies were now with him. The Administration at Washington had placed the full measure of its confidence in his leadership, and he now occupied a position that only two men before him had held: Washington and Scott.

Sometimes a despatch from one of our armies would reach us at 8 or 9 o'clock; sometimes it would be nearly midnight, and again at a still later hour. I had to take the message and translate it, and this was no child's play. Oftentimes I crawled into bed at 2 o'clock in the morning. I don't want to convey the impression that I was busy every night translating reports until wearied with work I sought my cot for a few hours rest; by no means. But I had enough to do in preparing despatches and deciphering those that came in over the wire to keep me occupied a portion of every evening. When I wasn't employed in this manner I was doing other things that had to be done by one who was cipher operator, clerk and secretary to the commanding General all in one.

I occupied a little hut after our tents were abandoned a short distance from Grant's "cottage," and it was substantial if not of elaborate proportions. It measured about 10 feet by 12 and contained my cot, a desk, a couple of stools and a box as furniture equipment. Into the rear wall was built a fireplace, and when the days grew short and the nights long the cheerful light from the log wood, supplementing the candle flame, made my quarters fairly comfortable. The comradery of the camp was wholesome and pleasant and our latchkeys hung on the outside of the doors.

I am not loyalist enough to believe that Gen. Grant was always at work on military problems. No man could have endured such incessant and prolonged labor without respite. His mind must have demanded some surcease from care and he must have supplied the demand. The charge has been made that he sought relaxation in drink. I never saw him under the influence of liquor during all the months I was with him, and I am of the opinion that very few had a better opportunity to observe him than had I. In fact I can recall only one instance when I was a witness to his indulgence in liquor of any kind.

It was on the return trip from Philadelphia on the morning of the 15th of April, 1865, the day after the assassination of President Lincoln. Then Gen. F. T. Dent, his brother-in-law, purchased a pint of champagne in the Quaker City and the two drank it on the train on the way to Washington. If the accusation were true, which it is not, then it certainly was a pity that the brand of whiskey was not known, so a barrel of it, as the President put it, could have been sent to every officer in the field.

But Grant spent many hours alone and, I imagine, in quiet reflection, surrounded by the fragrant smoke of his cigar. He was quite a reader too, and though of course we didn't carry an extensive library with us books were by no means curiosities. One night the General came to my tent shortly before 2 o'clock.

"Beckwith," he said, "I want to borrow a couple of candles. I've exhausted my supply."

"Aren't you about ready for bed?" I asked as I proceeded to hunt up the articles wanted.

"Not yet," he answered. "I've got a book here that I want to finish before I lay it aside. You needn't sit up any longer, however. I don't believe I'll need you."

I undressed and blew out my light. I knew very well that he wouldn't require my services again, for having begun the volume and become interested in it he would stick to it until daylight, if necessary, in order to read it through. That was characteristic of the man.

There was one never ending source of affliction and entertainment at camp, and it was visitors. They came early and late, in summer and fall and winter, and they were a cosmopolitan lot. Some were the idly curious, who prowled around devouring with their eyes everything worth the seeing, and particularly Gen. Grant. Others insisted on hunting up this much pestered officer and being presented; and this was an ordeal that sorely tried the patience of that very patient individual. Occasionally he escaped without much affliction; frequently he was assailed by a fusillade of imbecile questions that would drive him into speedy and welcome seclusion.

There were ministers, doctors, lawyers, Congressmen, State officials, women who were hero worshippers and "delegations from the Almighty," as Lincoln described them. There were also those wiseacres who possessed exclusive knowledge of the way to put down the rebellion and who were anxious to disclose the fact; and the ubiquitous patriots, who had preferred to remain at home when the call was sent forth and who now were criticising the fellows who carried the guns. They were all there, and I came to recognize them on sight.

I remember a party of clergymen who descended upon City Point one day in August, I think it was, who were typical of these busybodies. They came upon the usual mission; they were looking for Grant and they wouldn't rest content until they had found him. They were introduced to him just outside of his tent and at once they proceeded to draw upon his closely locked fund of personal opinion.

"General," inquired one who wore spectacles and sideburns, "do you get very angry when you fight?"

"No, never was angry in my life," was the cool reply.

"But, General," he persisted, "don't you occasionally lose your temper when you are in battle?"

"No, haven't any temper," snapped Grant.

That seemed to satisfy the questioner and he subsided, but another immediately succeeded him.

"General," he asked, "who do you consider the greatest of our generals?"

"Sherman," was the quick response.

After their departure Grant turned to me and said:

"Beckwith, I wish you'd keep those people away from me; "they're a nuisance."

So I added to my other duties that of human barrier between the hard worked soldier and the persistent inquisitors that hovered about us ready to pounce upon the General whenever the chance presented itself.

Another amusing incident that occurred shortly afterward happened in my own quarters and was substantially as follows. Three prominent gentlemen of the cloth, the Rev. Dr. Corey of Utica, N. Y.; a Mr. Turner of Illinois and a Mr. Breckenridge of somewhere else, sought me out and desired to see the Lieutenant-General. I had been given my orders, as I have narrated above; but the standing of these visitors and my acquaintance with one of them were such that I didn't like to chase them away too abruptly. I bade them await my return, accordingly, and I hurried over to Grant to inform him of the trio's mission. Dr. Corey evidently mistrusted my good intentions, for he started out himself to find the object of his quest and began with the mess tent, the fly of which he raised and peered within. His companions, however, possessed more Spartan faith and remained behind.

Foreseeing a tiresome interview, the General adopted strategy.

"I'll go to them," he said, and rising he followed me back and entering unannounced he leaned complacently against the centre pole of my tent.

The two ministers, one a Congregationalist and the other a Baptist, had become involved in a heated dogmatical argument and paid no attention whatever to our arrival. They certainly did not recognize Grant, because there was nothing about him to denote his rank. He wore a soldier's blouse without a coat, his trousers were tucked into his boots, a black felt hat was on his head and he was smoking the stub of a cigar; surely a makeup that was a complete disguise to any one who didn't know him. We stood there for perhaps half a minute, while the debaters waxed warm over the knotty point at issue. Then I announced, "Gentlemen, the Lieutenant-General!"

There was no response; no cessation of the argument.

"Gentlemen," I shouted, "the Lieutenant-General!"

They stopped and looked from me to Grant and then around them in search of the very distinguised personage named. Suddenly it seemed to dawn on them that the humble and silent little man before them was the great leader. They jumped to their feet with hands extended with profuse expressions of delight.

That interview lasted just about three minutes. Grant didn't sit down: he spoke a few words, excused himself, bade them good day and was gone. Time was too precious to waste in idle conversation, and besides the General was a mighty poor conversationalist.

I have stated that some of our visitors were men of prominence in State and national affairs, and these generally came to City Point not as curious spectators but as interested observers to study the progress of the campaign and to confer with the Federal commanders.

In the spring of 1865 Secretary of State Seward visited headquarters and paid me the honor of a business call. I was sitting in my tent when he entered with an important despatch in his hand and requested me to put it into cipher for transmission by telegraph. He had a lighted cigar in his mouth, but asked me for a match, which I fished from my pocket and gave to him. When he found that he didn't need it he slipped it into his vest pocket. I invited him to take a seat, but he declined with a shake of the head and remained standing while I glanced over the telegram. Possibly Horace Greeley could have devised a worse scrawl than that upon the paper, but I know of no other intelligent being that would have been guilty of its authorship.

For several minutes I attempted to translate the message; it was a task too difficult for my poor powers.

"Mr. Secretary," I explained at length, "I guess my eyesight is bad to-day; I have been using it a great deal lately. I can't make this out."

He sat down with an amused twinkle in his eyes and seeing a cipher despatch on my table that I had prepared for Consul-General Patten of Montreal he inquired if he might look at it. I gave him permission and he picked it up, scanning it gravely for some time. Then he laid it down with the remark: "Humph! Beckwith, we don't seem to be able to read each other's writing." He then gave me his version of the hieroglyphics.

As I recall Mr. Seward he was a man of medium height and of a somewhat slender frame. His shoulders had a slight stoop, as if the burden bearing had been just a little bit too heavy. He had gray hair, and a great deal of it about the ears and the back of the head, and his face was that of a statesman, of my conception of a statesman, perhaps; the nose was very prominent, the mouth large and firm, the eyes calm and kindly with thick, beetling brows above them; preeminently an intellectual cast of features. He wore neither beard nor mustache.

Every man has his weakness, so they way, and Seward was no exception to the rule. The chief defect in his character was an overweening conceit, a well developed egotism that prompted the conviction that he and he alone was the Moses destined by the Almighty to lead the broken Union out of the wilderness of fraternal strife. It took Lincoln many months to convince him that the Almighty had called another; but he succeeded at last, and the truth was pressed home gently but firmly that he whom the nation had chosen for its leader, who came from out the West, undisciplined and uncultured, was in fact the leader of his people.

VIII. News of Victories.

The siege of Petersburg was, it is true, marked by none too brilliant achievements, but fortunately there were compensating victories elsewhere that fuelled the fires of Union enthusiasm and thrilled Northern hearts with joy. And, indeed, it was the salvation of the nation, this Federal success in other sections of the country, for had it not come to enkindle the waning hope and patriotism of our citizenship the chances were that Lincoln would have been defeated and a dishonorable peace been declared.

Providence has been very good to us during our 137 years of history, and I believe that one of the best manifestations of His fostering care of this republic is that in His own wise way He made it possible that the strong hand of "Father Abraham" held fast the wheel while the ship of state was tossing about on the waters of disunion.

How well I recall the throb of exultation I experienced when early in the evening of September 4, 1864, Sherman's despatch reached City Point announcing the capture of Atlanta. We knew that he had undertaken a monumental task, but we all had absolute confidence in his masterly generalship, and we were expecting to hear some favorable news of his prowess. Our expectations were realized. It was like a ray of warming sunshine bursting through the clouds of uncertainty that towered above us.

As soon as I had deciphered the gladsome message I hurried to Grant's quarters, well knowing the immense relief these words would cause him. There were two or three officers in the tent, I think that Rawlins was one of them, as I walked over to the General and handed him the translation. He read it through, silently at first, and then, in a loud voice and with much satisfaction, he informed his companions of the contents. They greeted the announcement with a cheer. Of course the news spread like wildfire and the rejoicing soon became general.

A few minutes afterward Grant delivered to me his historic reply. Here it is just as he wrote it:

(Cipher.)   HEAD QUARTERS ARMIES OF THE UNITED STATES,
CITY POINT, Va., Sept. 4, 1864.

Major-Gen. Sherman, Atlanta, Ga.

I have just received your dispatch announcing the capture of Atlanta. In honor of your great victory I have ordered a salute to be fired with shotted guns from every battery bearing upon the enemy. The salute will be fired within an hour amidst great rejoicing.

U. S. GRANT,
Lt. Gen.

The time mark on the message, 9 P. M., is in my own writing. I always noted the exact hour and minute at which a despatch was placed in my hands.

When the Federal cannon, pursuant to Grant's orders, belched their approval of the inauguration of the famous march to the sea, the enemy must have heard in the thunders of our artillery the voice of doom that heralded the downfall of the Confederacy.

Two weeks later Sheridan in the battle of Winchester emphatically defeated Gen. Early and sent his army whirling through the valley. The announcement of his success he wired to headquarters; and naturally it occasioned a repetition of the jubilation that was provoked by Sherman's message.

I know that Grant derived peculiar gratification from this demonstration of Little Phil's ability, because he had virtually gone sponsor for that commander's efficiency. The War Department had been very reluctant to entrust Sheridan with weighty responsibility, because of his youth—he was only 33 years old at this time—and had opposed his promotion to higher rank although conceding his fighting qualities. Now he had vindicated his superior's championship of his merit. He had made good and had proved that a boy in the saddle can lead an army.

Immediately on receipt of the telegram Grant ordered a hundred guns to be fired from each of the armies and forwarded cordial congratulations to the young officer. To Stanton he sent this recommendation:

(Cipher.)   HEAD QUARTERS ARMIES OF THE UNITED STATES,
                           CITY POINT, Va., Sept. 20, 1864.

Hon. E. M. Stanton, Sec. of War.

Let me urge now the appointment of Gen. Sheridan as Brig.-Gen. in the regular Army. Please also direct the promulgation of the order appointing him permanently to the Command of the Middle Division.

                                   U. S. GRANT,
                                   Lt. Gen

In response to request and as a recognition of his timely service to the nation, President Lincoln, through his War Secretary, made Sheridan a brigadier-general; and after the battle of Cedar Creek in November appointed him a major-general.

There was one noteworthy characteristic of Gen. Grant which perhaps I should mention at this point. It was his invariable habit to consult no one as to the composition of his despatches. Often when I went to him with a message of great importance there would be several of his generals present; I have seen Meade and Hancock and Burnside and others in his tent or cabin at various times on such occasions. But he would submit his reply to none of them for approval. He usually read the telegram that I delivered to him carefully, and if a response were required he turned to his desk and wrote it out without hesitancy. Sometimes, if the matter required greater deliberation, he would bring it to me himself a half hour or so later. I don't mean to say that he did not advise with his officers as to the conduct of the campaign; I mean that rarely did any one except himself and me read his despatches before transmission. He was the master whose mind directed the movements of the army.

Grant and Lincoln were very unlike in their manner of writing. The former wrote with careless speed. He paid no attention to punctuation and frequently violated the proprieties of spelling and grammar, as will be discovered by an examination of his letters and telegrams, the facsimiles of some of which illustrate these memoirs. These are all photographed from the originals which were preserved by me after their receipt. A schoolboy of academic grade can readily detect the errors committed by the writer. It is true that Grant was not a wonderful literary genius, but I am sure that these mistakes were due to haste and not to ignorance.

Lincoln, on the other hand, took more pains with the pen. I have stood beside him many times while he composed messages to his generals and officials. He was much more deliberate in putting his thoughts together and he seemed to study the phraseology with considerable attention. He employed punctuation marks freely; and while the handwriting is not as legible as Grant's, the composition, I presume, would stand scrutiny better.

Gen. Grant was not, however, careless in the preservation of his papers and corespondence. I acted as a sort of clerk as well as operator at headquarters, and was entrusted with the duty of keeping his desk in order. The task was by no means arduous. He never questioned my unqualified integrity and he had no documents that were hidden from my eyes. Was it weakness upon my part that I was immensely pleased with his faith in me?

In the fore part of December Grant's anxiety for some decisive movement on the part of Thomas became very manifest. It will be recalled that the Federal forces under the command of the latter officer had retired behind their intrenchments at Nashville, while Hood, with his Army of the Tennessee, had taken up his position before the city with high hopes of crushing his opponent.

It was the expectation of Grant that his indomitable General would quickly overwhelm the enemy and bring another of his splendid triumphs to the Union arms. Many critics have never been able to justify his extreme impatience with the deliberation of Thomas. The hitherto uniformly successful career of this able soldier did not now seem to be sufficient assurance of victory. In view of the repeated reverses sustained by our troops around Petersburg the persistent demands made by Grant for immediate action and the almost petulance displayed over the non-compliance with his orders, I am frank to admit, impressed me at the time as being rather strange. And yet I presume that the failures of the Army of the Potomac stirred him to a keen realization of the imperative necessity for substantial successes elsewhere.

During the first two weeks of the month Grant fairly bombarded Thomas with telegrams urging him to attack Hood. The tenor of all the replies was the same. He was getting ready to move as soon as he could. He was making preparations. He would take the offensive when prepared.

Few armies have had to contend with such execrable weather conditions as had the Union army in Nashville. The ground was a field of almost impassable ice, making military operations practically impossible. The Federal commander was tied hand and foot by ungovernable circumstances; but Grant apparently believed that he could and should conquer both the elements and the enemy, and the continued delay finally instigated him to drastic measures.

If my memory serves me right no day went by that he did not place in my hands a despatch for Thomas. I could easily see that he was greatly worried over the situation, and every night he would await the news of an engagement with much concern. When a telegram from Nashville was delivered to me that contained no cheering news of a forward movement I felt deeply the disappointment it would cause him and occasionally I forewarned him of the contents by saying as I entered the room, "No battle yet, General."

In the afternoon of December 11 Grant wired Thomas as follows:
"If you delay attack longer the mortifying spectacle will be witnessed of a rebel army moving from the Ohio River, and you will be forced to act, accepting such weather as you find. Let there be no further delay. Hood cannot even stand a drawn battle so far from his supplies of ordnance stores. If he retreats and you follow he must lose his artillery and much of his army. I am in hopes of receiving a despatch from you to-day announcing that you have moved. Delay no longer for weather or reenforcements."

But the longed for despatch did not come. Major-Gen. Logan was at City Point at this time, and Grant in despair directed him to proceed to Nashville to relieve Thomas and to keep the order secret until his arrival. Then if the battle was on to consider the order revoked. Logan started for Tennessee, but the General was not content. His uneasiness of mind was revealed in his drawn features. He could not understand the disinclination of his subordinate to risk a combat when the chances were more than even that he would beat Hood. A Fabian policy was wholly foreign to his style of playing the game.

When about 9 o'clock on the evening of the 14th no word came from Nashville that the army had taken the initiative Grant came to my quarters with a look of finality on his face.

"Beckwith," he said, "you've got just fifteen minutes to pack your knapsack and get on that boat. Hustle."

I knew what that meant. He was going to the front himself to take personal charge of the army of Thomas. In less than half an hour we were on board of the General's special despatch boat, the Mary Martin, and upon our way to Washington. Grant's baggage was not very cumbersome. It consisted, as I recall it, of a pocket full of cigars. I don't believe that he carried any luggage. Mine was hardly more extensive, although I did provide myself with a few articles of wearing apparel.

On the journey north there was little or no conversation between us. He had definitely decided upon a course of action, and there being no official business to transact talk was unnecessary. That, in short, was Grant's habit of silence. He was never designed by the Creator for a sociable being, at least so far as I ever learned from observation and experience. I had become accustomed to his moods, however, and I left him alone to his meditations while I sought a few hours of much needed sleep.

We arrived at the capital the next day, the 15th, in the early afternoon, and went at once to the Willard. Grant directed me to remain at the hotel until his return and hurried away to the War Department to confer with Secretary Stanton. There was no news from Thomas. The wires running into Nashville for some reason were temporarily out of commission, and in consequence not a word had come to the eager watchers of the struggle that was under way.

That evening in the War Secretary's office was held a conference between Stanton, Mr. Lincoln, Halleck and Grant at which the last named General condemned the inactivity of Thomas and demanded his immediate removal. I learned subsequently that he also wrote out his third order of dismissal and gave it to Major Eckert for transmission to Nashville, which order that official upon his own responsibility withheld pending some word from the front.

The very reliable Bates in his "Lincoln in the Telegraph Office" says that at 11 o'clock a despatch came from Van Duzer to the War Department containing the welcome intelligence of Federal victory, a copy of which was sent to Grant at the Willard.[24]

My recollection of events may not be perfect, but I believe that my friend is slightly in error. I know that I lingered about the hotel all the evening awaiting the reappearance of my superior with considerable impatience. I thought at the time that if the General was anxious for an attack upon Hood he was somewhat deliberate in his own progress toward Nashville. It was along toward midnight when he returned to the hotel, and I noticed that his face wore a smile of satisfaction that betokened good tidings. He came to me directly and there was a note of cordiality in his voice that had been missing for many a day as he said:

"Beckwith, I guess that we won't go to Nashville after all. Thomas has licked Hood."

I am reasonably certain that he had received the news of the victory at the Department, where naturally he would expect that the despatches would be sent. He was not the man to seek his bed until something definite had reached him of the day's events.

To J. C. Van Duzer, superintendent of military telegraphs of the Department of the Cumberland, belongs the distinction of flashing to Washington the first word of the battle. At half past 10 o'clock on the night of the 15th, he wired that Thomas had assailed Hood that morning and had driven him in headlong rout a distance of eight miles. This message followed closely the General's own announcement that "the ice having melted away to-day, the enemy will be attacked to-morrow," a despatch written early in the evening of the 14th, but held up because of the disarranged telegraph service.

Of course Grant was greatly pleased at this sweeping success. He immediately sent his slow but sure commander congratulations and urged him "to push the enemy now and give him no rest until he is entirely destroyed," an injunction which Thomas carried out with relentless perseverance. The "Rock of Chickamauga" had become the "Sledge of Nashville." We returned to Petersburg in a much more cheerful frame of mind. That stronghold must now fall.

24. Bates, 316.

IX. A Few Snapshots. Rawlins.

By virtue of my position and of my intimacy with Gen. Grant I had cordial acquaintance with many of the prominent men who assisted in the making of history in the earlier '60s. In this chapter I wish to turn the spotlight of memory upon two soldiers whose work has been done and whose course has been run these many years.

The name of Major-Gen. John A. Rawlins may not be familiar to the average reader of to-day, but in me it revives most pleasurable and tender recollections. Rawlins was Gen. Grant's chief of staff and during his first Presidential term his Secretary of War.

Perhaps in the first place I ought to say something about the personnel o[f] that staff over which the whole souled John A. presided. To tell the simple truth, I don't suppose it would have taken first prize in an official contest of intelligence and ability, for they who constituted it were an aggregation of good fellows who had been selected by Grant largely because of personal friendship. I don't mean to say that good fellowship was their only asset by any means, for the majority of them capably discharged their duties; but had the criterion of membership been intellectual and physical fitness alone some would probably have fallen below the standard.

It is probably true that there were one or two members of the staff who took some slight advantage of the General's friendship for them by idleness and an occasional indulgence in liquor. They were men who owed their places to pull or long acquaintanceship; and the result was merely what may always be expected when fitness and adaptability are ignored. But there were others, and they were in a decided majority, who were thoroughly competent officials and a credit to the commander they served. Col. T. S. Bowers, the staff judge advocate, was an excellent officer; so also Cols. Wilson, the Inspector-General; Comstock, chief engineer; Kent, provost marshal; Ely S. Parker, a full-blooded Indian, the military secretary, and later promoted for efficiency, and most assuredly Rawlins.

John A. Rawlins in 1863 was about 32 years of age. He was a Westerner and a lawyer, and consequently well able to handle himself in argument and "speechifying." Grant first took a fancy to him at a public meeting held at Galena, Ill., shortly after Fort Sumter was fired upon and over which the future leader of the Federal armies presided. The young attorney at that time took the floor and delivered a ringing patriotic address that elicited enthusiastic applause and captivated both his audience and the chairman. Thenceforward acquaintance developed friendship and friendship engendered comradeship of the most sincere nature.

Grant found in Rawlins that alter ego which is best described by that homely term, pal. Between them existed a mutual understanding and genuine regard that gave license to untrammelled familiarity. It was no novel thing to hear the zealous subordinate administer to his superior a stiff verbal castigation because of some act that met the former's stern disapproval. And Grant never resented any reprimand bestowed upon him by Rawlins. He knew it was prompted by an ardent anxiety for his own welfare and by a loyalty that was unwavering.

At headquarters the lawyer soldier was boss, and his title was conceded by every one. He had no very extensive book learning, which sometimes is a misfortune; but he had a fund of practical education that well equipped him for his position. His vocabulary was frequently picturesque and unrighteous; and he didn't hesitate to visit his ornamental wrath upon dignitary and menial alike. He was not awed by personality. I have heard it said that Rawlins and Sherman could outswear any two officers in the army.

My duties naturally threw me into constant intercourse with headquarters staff and I harbored a warm affection for this rough and ready soldier. He was a hard worker and he wasn't at all particular about the number of hours in his working day. The night had no terrors for him. His figure was slight and his health none too robust; his large black eyes and flushed cheeks giving one an impression of some latent weakness that sooner or later would have its toll. He died in September, 1869, and I am sure that all who knew him, and they were legion, mourned sincerely his untimely death. And of them all none must have felt more deeply the loss of Rawlins, though doubtless that feeling was obvious to no one, than Grant, his comrade and friend.

Major-Gen. Richard J. Oglesby I had known when he was a colonel, and I had followed his career with a great deal of satisfaction. While with Wallace I had ample opportunity to become acquainted with this Prince of Good Fellows; for almost every evening he would drop into our headquarters and spend an hour or two, oftentimes several hours, with my superior. At such times he would entertain not only the General but all who happened to be present with his joyial conversation. He was a first rate story teller and had been an extensive traveller, a combination of natural ability and experience that certainly produced wholesome diversion. I have occasionally listened to his amusing narrations until 3 o'clock in the morning, when he would yawn, solicitously inquire the time and, pretending an apology, bid us a hasty good night. He was a panacea for all mental ills, and his cheery disposition shed a radiance wherever he went.

Oglesby was constructed on somewhat generous lines. He was only 5 feet 8 inches tall, but he weighed pretty close to 190 pounds. Fat and good nature, they say, always go together; and in his case the saying held true. We used to joke him on the subject of his avoirdupois, but he always gave us as good as he received and maintained that physical and mental weight went together.

"Uncle Dick" the boys called him, and he was immensely popular with men and officers. And this popularity in after years, coupled with unquestionable ability, secured for him high place in public life. He was elected

Governor of Illinois in 1865 and again, twenty years later, in 1885. In 1873 he was sent to the United States Senate. He died in April, 1899, and when his genial spirit passed away from earth, the good St. Peter must have opened wide the gates, recognizing in him one who had scattered sunshine along life's pathway with prodigal generosity. And, after all, I imagine that Paradise is peopled with that kind of souls.

When we were at Cairo, one day shortly after the battle of Belmont, Oglesby and I were looking at a projectile that had been brought to the city and placed on exhibition. It was a huge shell, almost three feet in length and as big around as a man's thigh. He surveyed it for some time apparently deep in thought.

Then patting his abdominal rotundity, he said:

"Suppose, Beckwith, that one of those things should get inside of a fellow and bust; what a devil of a stomach ache it would cause him."

Bravery was so native to the commanders on both sides of the rebellion that to say Gen. Oglesby was brave would be a needless assertion. It was inevitable. At Fort Donelson I saw him riding furiously along the ranks of his command, waving his hat above his head and cheering on his men, reckless of the danger that hurtled about him. In the battle of Corinth he was equally fearless, exposing himself to the fire of the enemy with the utmost composure and receiving a wound that necessitated his retirement from the engagement.

As soon as I could steal away from my duties I went over to the hospital to see how seriously damaged the brave fellow was. He was surrounded by a group of nurses and surgeons, who had stripped off his shirt and were examining his wound. It was by no means fatal, the bullet having penetrated the fleshy part of the shoulder, leaving the bones intact. I was genuinely glad that he had so fortunately escaped. Going to his side, I scrutinized him with mock gravity and remarked:

"General, if you hadn't been so fat that bullet would surely have hit you."

He glared at me for a moment in assumed anger; then waving the nurses away, he called me a hardened wretch and laughed goodnaturedly over his predicament.

X. The War Correspondent.

The newspaper plant of rebellion years was not, I assume, the perfect machine that to-day collects and disseminates news the world over, but it was sufficiently developed to give to an eager public satisfying accounts of the activities of the armies in camp and battle. Naturally during the period from 1861 to 1865 the country was alert for information from the front, and to supply the people with this desired information the larger journals had their chosen representatives to report first hand the issue between the States.

We who were connected with Gen. Grant's headquarters were in a position to see much of these industrious correspondents. They came and went, bearing with them descriptions of various engagements and sieges, many of which were more or less colored by their indispensable imaginations. At times, I will acknowledge, some of these reporters were plain downright nuisances. They didn't hesitate to enter my tent and rummage among the papers on my desk for information which they could gain in no honorable way. I was obliged more than once to order them out and administer a stiff reprimand for their intolerable presumption. I understand that such methods are countenanced to-day by certain journals on the theory that what is good for the public to know should be procured by hook or by crook, and they condone the offence by calling it enterprise.

Well, one thing is certain, and it is that such enterprise received mighty little encouragement from Rawlins and his associates at headquarters. There are many things going on in war time that the Government must temporarily keep secret, and it was my duty as virtual private secretary to the commanding General to see that no confidential matters in his and my keeping were disclosed. I think that I discharged that duty reasonably well too.

My first experience with a newspaper man was much to my liking, and if others had only followed his commendable example I imagine I could have developed quite an affection for them. It was at the close of the second day at the battle of Corinth, when for the first time the terrible reality of grim war was heavy upon me. I had been a witness of the desperate charges of the brave Confederates upon batteries Williams and Robinett, I had seen them mowed down like standing grain before the scythe by the Federal artillery, and in the seclusion of my tent I was trying to figure out the meaning of all this bloodshed.

I was interrupted by the unannounced entrance of a man who looked as if he had seen some hard travelling. He introduced himself as the representative of the Chicago *Tribune* and inquired anxiously if any other correspondent had arrived at the front. When I told him that he was the first and only reporter to reach us since the battle began he was greatly relieved. He wanted an account of the fight; would I give it to him?

Candidly it was a privilege for me to sit down beside him and unburden myself of the story of the engagement. He could have come to no better source of information, for I had been since the first gun was fired an interested spectator of events. For an hour or more I gave him what I believed must have been a pretty graphic narration, and when I was done he thanked me profusely. He also did what appealed to me more strongly than mere gratitude; from his wallet he took $50 in lawful money of the United States and handed it to me as a mark of appreciation. Permit me to remark that it was duly appreciated, for my exchequer was sadly depleted at the time. The *Tribune* the following morning had an exceptionally fine story of the battle, and it was, if my memory serves me right, a clear "scoop."

There was only one representative of any of the metropolitan papers who made his permanent headquarters with us, and he was a scribe who answered to the name of Cadwallader. That is, Cadwallader was his lawful and rightful cognomen; he answered usually to the name of "Cad," for that was the sobriquet thrust upon him by Grant's officers. As men average up he was among the choicest of God's amiable creatures, a whole souled, affable gentleman who carried with him quite a store of the optimism of life which he shed around him. The matter of fact Rawlins had developed a strong liking for him, and hence "Cad" was persona grata in camp, for any one who bore the stamp of John A.'s indorsement was admitted to the comradeship of our official family. I very much doubt if "the boss" would have tolerated any other reporter about staff quarters, for he had little patience with interlopers.

One reason for our adoption of Cadwallader was that we could trust him. He never went snooping around our private "apartments" in quest of items of news which we desired to withhold from publication, and when he did acquire information in camp circles which he knew was not for the press he played the game fairly and didn't abuse the confidence we had in him.

And let me say right here that "Cad" knew his business. He had his own tent and equipment and plenty of money, and he had besides that valuable asset that is so prized by journalists, the news instinct. As I recall it, he had been associated with the Chicago *Times*, but had been drafted by the New York *Herald*, and in 1864 was the chief representative of that paper in the field. The *Herald* had men also at Meade's and Butler's headquarters before Petersburg, but they were subordinate to Cadwallader, to whom they reported for instructions.

We had a good joke on our genial friend at one time, although it was rather an expensive one and probably not so keenly appreciated by him as by ourselves. Col. Duff of Grant's staff had a remarkably fine horse that attracted the discriminating eye of Cadwallader. The latter needed a mount in the discharge of his labors, so a dicker was made between him and Duff whereby the animal became the property of the *Herald* man for $400 in cash. "Cad" was immensely proud of his purchase and contemplated it with beaming approval.

The very next day, however, the Confederate raider, the redoubtable Mosby, captured the "critter" and its owner never saw it again. It lived only in his memory. Some of the boys tried to persuade him that Duff was a party to a conspiracy to deprive him of his treasured possession, but their efforts were vain.

Being a correspondent Cadwallader was inevitably of a loquacious nature. He was telling Gen. Grant one afternoon about his narrow escape from compulsory service in the army. It appeared that his occupation of newspaper man had been no protection to him from the draft, as he had been drawn for duty some time before.

"But," he chuckled, "I got out of it nicely. I bought a nigger to take my place."

Grant puffed his cigar thoughtfully for a moment while he surveyed "Cad" from top to bottom.

"Perhaps," he remarked dryly, "the army profited by the exchange."

I asked Cadwallader after the laugh had subsided how he would have liked me for a substitute.

The General winked at Rawlins, who was one of the group.

"I suppose," said he, "you think that if you went as his substitute we here would have to get you detailed to headquarters again. Don't be so sure of that, Beckwith."

I knew from his manner that the words were a covert compliment to my faithfulness to him, and I am persuaded to my own satisfaction, at least, that it was precisely what he would have done if such an improbable thing had happened. I assured him, however, that I was well contented with my lot.

The meeting of Lincoln and Sheridan at City Point after the Shenandoah raid has been broadly published; but only in part, I believe, have the particulars of that interesting occasion been disclosed. I happened to be a witness of the Presidential congratulation, and consequently can speak intelligently on the subject. Of course, there is no great historical importance attached to the occurrence; but it is, in a way, memorable because it is a contribution to the mass of incident that reveals the character of the illustrious participants.

Gen. Sheridan had sent his cavalry around to White House for the purpose of having his horses reshod and the troopers refurnished with necessary supplies. He himself rode over to City Point with Capt. Forsyth, his chief of staff.

President Lincoln, who, at the time of Sheridan's arrival, was upon the River Queen, where he slept nights, learned from his son Robert that the little General was in camp. As a matter of fact, quite a number of celebrities were congregated in the tent of Col. Bowers; and I, who happened to be at leisure for the moment, made a humble and interested member of the group.

Gen. W. T. Sherman was pointing out on a map which hung on the rear "flap" of the tent his route from Atlanta to Savannah, by which his 60,000 "Yankee boys" had carried the old flag through the heart of the Confederacy. Gen. George Meade, the hero of Gettysburg, stood beside him, following his finger as it traced the line of march. A few feet away and watching intently the demonstration, but making no comment, was Sheridan.

The contrast between these noted men was striking. Sherman was then in the flush of his vigorous manhood, 44 years of age and as hard as nails. He was lean, tall and wiry. His face was sun tanned, bearded with a scrub growth of sandy hair and full of lively expression. The eyes were blue and penetrating;

the cheek and brow furrowed by experience's telltale lines. His manner was nervous, his language forceful.

Meade resembled a Spaniard, and in fact he was born in Cadiz, Spain, in 1815. He was therefore five years Sherman's senior; and he certainly looked it. His face was very thin, his cheeks hollow, his complexion somewhat sallow. He had black eyes that appeared rather lustreless behind the spectacles. He wore a mustache and a modest beard.

Gen. Phil Sheridan was a midget. He weighed only 140 pounds at this time and was short of stature, being 5 feet 4½ inches in height. One would hardly have picked him out as the dashing cavalry leader whose fame had now spread world wide, but something in his rough, manly face indicated unique character and courage. One sensed a latent force that the smoke and fire of battle called into invincible action. He was comparatively a young man (he was but 33 years of age), and he showed a becoming deference to his older comrades. He wore an ordinary service coat and a small brown hat; and, like his companions, was without sword or belt or gloves.

While the lecture was in progress the towering form of Lincoln entered the tent ("towering" I use advisedly, his stovepipe hat bringing his altitude pretty close to the 7 foot mark). He walked over to Little Phil and extended his huge hand in greeting. Sheridan, nonplussed, perfunctorily responded.

"I used to think at the beginning of the war," said the President, shaking the General's hand with great heartiness, 'that a cavalry leader should be 6 feet 4 inches in height. I have changed my mind"—still shaking the hand and beaming down upon the soldier—"5 feet 4 will do very well."

I thought that the handshaking process was going to last interminably, so cordial and buoyant was the warmth of Lincoln's greeting. Throughout it all Sheridan said not a word; he stood like a schoolboy before the master, his face suffused with a modest blush. And when "Uncle Abe" abruptly turned on his heel and left the tent the little General remained apparently transfixed, while Sherman continued his recital of his march to the sea. I did not hear him utter a syllable of comment on the flattering honor that had been paid him.

XI. Abraham Lincoln.

Abraham Lincoln was, I believe, the greatest man this country has produced. I did not, of course, have the opportunity of knowing the President that I had of knowing Grant; but I enjoyed several days of rare intimacy and came to esteem and revere him. I realize that a wealth of story has been told about him and that I can add little of interest to the abundance; hence my contribution will be brief.

Grant had a wholesome liking and respect for Lincoln. They seemed, each of them, thoroughly to understand the other and to trust the other implicitly.

The Administration had been trying out men as Generals in a resolute endeavor to find the man who could bring victory to the Union arms and end the war within a reasonable time. The experiment had proved costly and discouraging. McDowell, McClellan, Pope, Burnside and Hooker had been given the chance to make good and they had failed. Even Meade, after the splendid success of Gettysburg, seemed to rest content with his laurels and fall short of the measurements demanded.

Gen. Grant's successes in the West had stamped him with the mark of genius. He was selected as Lincoln's last hope, and when the President knew his worth and saw his handiwork, he placed the army in his keeping and backed the intrepid soldier in his every move. And Grant appreciated highly the cooperation and loyal support given him from Washington. Unlike McClellan and his successors, he did not bombard the Capitol with petitions and remonstrances and criticisms and appeals for reenforcements. He knew that the country was sending him all the men available; he knew that he had the confidence of the Executive and his Cabinet; he knew what was expected of him; and he did it as best, as quickly as he could, without complaint or boasting or vain display.

While there was no close friendship between Lincoln and his General, born of personal relationship and intercourse, there was a reciprocal regard that was perhaps even better. When the news of the President's reelection in November, 1864, reached City Point, Grant was deeply gratified. Naturally he construed the verdict of the people as a cordial ratification of his own leadership in the field, which was part and parcel of the Administration policy. He at once wrote a congratulatory message to Secretary Stanton and handed it to me in person for translation into cipher and transmission to Washington. It expressed his conception of the meaning and the results of Republican victory.

(Cipher.)   HEADQUARTERS ARMIES OF THE UNITED STATES,
CITY POINT, Va., Nov. 10, 1864.
Hon. E. M. Stanton, Sec. of War, Washington.

Enough now seems to be known to say who is to hold the reins of Government for the next four years. Congratulate the President for me for the double victory. The election having passed off quietly, no bloodshed or rioit (sic) throughout the land, is a victory worth more to the country than a battle won. Rebeldom and Europe will so construe it.

U. S. GRANT,
Lt. Gen.

I was not present at Lee's surrender at Appomattox April 9. Gen. Grant had assigned me to the President and I accompanied the latter on Admiral Porter's barge from Richmond to City Point. I was to keep him in touch by telegraph with the army in its advance movement and with the War Department at Washington. For the next two weeks out of the three yet remaining to him Lincoln was my constant employer. He would come over in the morning from the River Queen and take his seat at the desk which Col. Bowers had supplied him, and there he would sit most of the day waiting for news from the front. The telegraph office was in the hospital tent about 150 yards away. Whenever a message arrived directed to the President an orderly brought it to me, if it was in cipher, and I translated it as quickly as possible. This done I took it myself to Lincoln, always saluting as I presented it and awaiting orders. If it were a despatch that required an answer I would stand beside him while he slowly and methodically composed his reply, reading it over to see that he had correctly stated his ideas.

I was kept pretty busy with my official labors, for Mr. Lincoln was exceedingly anxious to secure information about everything of importance that was going on. Occasionally I would find him poring over a map of the State of Virginia and diligently tracing the positions of the armies. My tent was but a few feet from his own quarters and our neighborly situation developed a satisfying friendliness. It was a time when the last act of the war drama was drawing to its close, and naturally the heart of every Union man was filled with exultation. Father Abraham shared in full measure the spirit of thanksgiving and hopefulness. His lined and careworn face appeared to lose some of its native sadness and he looked forward, I am sure, with trust and confidence into the future. And certainly from his rounded shoulders a mighty burden was lifting.

The President was, of course, immensely popular with the soldiers everywhere. All of them, from the generals down to the privates, knew that in him they had a sympathetic friend, a kind and wise protector. The names bestowed upon him, "Uncle Abe," "Father Abraham," "Old Abe," and the like, were terms of genuine affection. The boys felt that he was with them and of them. Stories of his great tenderness of heart were common property of the camp, and the human side of this tall, ungainly, homely man brought him very close to us all.

As with Grant, awe of Lincoln's greatness did not oppress me. They were too genuine and democratic. But I realized then, at least looking back upon him through the years, I realize now the almost infinite depth and breadth of his mind and heart and soul.

It may seem improbable to my readers that in the presence of this wonderful man I did not feel a sense of awe, a consciousness of my own inferiority. The simple truth is that Uncle Abe did not inspire any such feeling in those who knew him. His manner was so candid and unaffected that you felt admitted into his brotherhood as an equal; at least you felt that he so wished it, which is perhaps just as good.

I was standing one day outside headquarter's tent, when the President came along in company with two or three officers. He stopped at my side and looked me over with a critical eye. Then throwing his arm about my neck and straightening up his lofty form so as to make the disparity in our heights the more noticeable (I am but 5 feet and 5 inches tall), he said to those present:

"Difference in stature, gentlemen, is not always indicative of difference in ability."

Then he slapped me cordially upon the back and with a chuckle passed into the tent.

It is not my intention to repeat incidents which are already familiar to my readers; hence I must omit from these memoirs many interesting experiences which I shared with President Lincoln during the two weeks that I served him as operator. Bates has drawn liberally upon my stock of reminiscences, and the residue is hardly worthy of preservation. I could write of the visit which Lincoln paid to Richmond on the 4th and 5th of April, when I accompanied him at his direction; but the history of that visit, in brief, has already been chronicled by my friend.[25] I could tell something of his wonderful facility in story telling; but that subject has been thoroughly exhausted. So you see that I am somewhat in the position of the man who has a great deal to relate, but having related it before, no one cares to listen.

When the Federal forces were closing in on Lee and the ragged army of the South was striving, like a desperately hunted stag, to elude its pursuer, Sheridan, whose cavalry was pounding at the enemy's tired feet, sent a hasty report to Grant, concluding with these words: "If the thing is pressed, I think that Lee will surrender." The General forwarded the despatch to Lincoln, who instantly replied: "Let the thing be pressed."

One of Col. Bowers's clerks took the laconic message to the telegraph office. He was very much impressed with its forceful brevity and asked the President if he might retain the original as a souvenir. The face of the nation's chief lightened up with a smile as he said:

"I guess, young man, that the document's yours. Possession is nine points of the law, you know."

I want to go outside of my own experiences for a moment to narrate an incident told me by Thomas Wheeler, ex-Mayor and present postmaster of Utica, a member of the fighting 146th New York and a soldier of unquestioned bravery. It is so illustrative of the fatherly kindness of the man that I feel it will well bear a place in these memoirs.

In the early summer of 1864, a very crucial period of the war, young Wheeler, then a lad of 19, was convalescing at Emory Hospital, in the city of Washington, from a serious illness. On a cot next to his was a soldier of a Pennsylvania regiment whose name was Ira Wing. Regularly every week a letter, sometimes two, came from Wing's home, conveying the distressing

25. *Ibid.*, 353–58.

tidings of his wife's rapidly declining health. She was a victim of consumption and her grip on life was daily weakening. Usually there was attached to each missive a pitiful little postscript in her handwriting, appealing to him to get a short leave of absence that she might bid him good-by before the end came.

The poor chap was unable to read or write, so his comrade read the letters to him, striving at the time as best he could to encourage him with cheering words. But the effort was futile; Wing was disconsolate.

"It was mighty tough," said Wheeler in telling the story, "and the worst of it was there didn't seem to be any relief in sight. We soldiers who were confined in the hospitals weren't privileged to go and come as we willed. We were still enlisted men and couldn't any more leave the capital without leave than we could our regiment in the field. And it wasn't an easy matter to secure permission to visit the city, either. Guards were patrolling the grounds and the streets, and a man in uniform wandering around without a permit generally had some explaining to do.

"Well, you can readily see that Wing was up against it. He tried to get a short furlough and failed. We were strangers in a strange clime, had no commanding officer at hand through whom we could apply and consequently we had to resort to the surgeon of the hospital, who, I imagine, paid about as much attention to such a petition as he did to an attack of toothache.

"It certainly was hard luck. There was the girl back there whom he had sworn to love and protect, and he did love her, wasting away like a late summer rose, and here was he, cooped up like a prisoner, idling away his time when the hours seemed so precious.

"Finally another letter came, and it was a heart breaker. She was worse, much worse, and she was asking for him. What was he to do? What would any one do under the circumstances? Desert—that was about all that was left, and it was desertion that he determined upon. He didn't care for results; he was going home and he was going to see her at all hazards.

"I tried to dissuade him from such a serious offence; he was desperate—and candidly I couldn't blame him. Then I began to figure out some other plan. I had oftentimes heard of President Lincoln's paternal interest in his soldier boys, and the thought occurred to me that if we could only get to him somehow all might be well yet. So I put the proposition up to Ira.

"'What, me see Lincoln!' he replied. 'We couldn't get within gunshot of him. He ain't bothering with such small fry as us. There's too much on his mind of bigger things.'

"I appreciated the probable truth of his remark, but I didn't want to see him court-martialled for desertion; so I kept at him. At last he consented to make the effort; he was willing to do most anything that offered a possible loophole of escape. The hospital steward, Frank McKeezie, was from Utica, and there was therefore a bond of friendship between us. I got a pass from him and the next morning Wing and I started for the White House.

"As I look back at it now the enterprise smacked of the presumption of youth and ignorance. We were two very obscure privates who had no other passport to the Executive Chamber than our extreme necessity, and the chances were strongly against any one examining that passport. The fates, however, were with us.

"We were several blocks from the White House when whom should I see coming down Pennsylvania avenue but tall and ungainly Uncle Abe himself. You couldn't mistake him if you saw him in Egypt. I turned to Wing.

" 'Here comes the President now. Don't be scared,' I suggested, 'and when we get up to him you nail him and tell him all about it.'

"My advice was good, but he was unequal to the occasion. As we approached the Executive his resolution oozed away like snow before an April sun, and when we were within speaking distance of him Wing was absolutely dumb. He couldn't have spoken a word if his life had depended on it. In the parlance of the day it was strictly up to me. I saluted.

" 'Mr. President,' I said.

"He saluted in turn, as he always did when meeting a soldier, and stopped.

" 'What is it, young man?' he asked.

"That was my opening. I screwed my courage to the sticking point and began to plead my case. I told him briefly the circumstances of my companion's plight, of his sickness and convalescence, of the letters that kept coming from home full of sad news about the little woman who, almost in the valley of the shadow, was longing day by day for the presence of her soldier husband. I told him of our effort to secure a leave of absence and our failure and then at last of his determination to desert.

"Mr. Lincoln's eyes, the saddest I have ever seen, seemed to me suspiciously moist as I unfolded to him our predicament; but when I mentioned the word 'desertion' his face took on a most fatherly sternness as, placing his big hand on the shoulder of my wondering comrade, he said:

" 'My boy, never desert your country in her hour of peril. She needs you and she needs us all. Her life depends upon the loyalty of men like you.'

"With that he took him by the arm; the President of the United States, upon whose wearied shoulders were then resting heavily the terrible burdens of that terrible conflict, and the humble private, and together we went to the office of the Military Governor or Commandant of the city—I am pretty sure that was the department visited. And what do you think 'Father Abraham' did for Ira and the wife? He drew six months back pay and gave it to him, and he got him a month's furlough besides.

" 'Now,' said he in parting, 'you go home to the woman's who's waiting for you. And if she still needs you when your month is up you let me know and I will see to it that your time is extended. I guess the country can spare you to her for a while.'

"Poor Wing! He couldn't express his thanks, but he looked it, and that was enough. Either of us would willingly have laid our lives at Lincoln's feet after that."

Mrs. Lincoln was at City Point during the last week of March with little Tad. I saw her frequently and somehow gained the idea that she was not of the same homely mould as was her husband. An incident which, at the time, struck me as rather significant of the fact occurred on the 6th of April, the day after we had returned from Richmond.

On the 1st of April, I believe it was, Mrs. Lincoln had gone to Washington, leaving her son at headquarters. She came back on the 6th, however, on a special boat, with a distinguished party, among whom were Senator Sumner and the Hon. James Harlan, Secretary of the Interior, and Mrs. Harlan. They were on their way to the captured city.

I was in the President's tent when Harlan entered and invited Lincoln to accompany them. He declined, saying that he had but just returned from there. Then said Harlan:

"I speak now as the messenger of Mrs. Lincoln. Your presence is desired on board. She wishes you to go with her to Richmond."

Lincoln arose. "If you are a messenger from Mrs. Lincoln," said he firmly, "take this message back from Mr. Lincoln. Tell her that if her boat doesn't start for Richmond in fifteen minutes, I'll take the River Queen and go back to Washington."

Now what did that mean? I inferred from the remarks and the manner in which he spoke, that it was intended as an ultimatum. I really believe that he considered it a mighty inappropriate time to be running sight seeing excursions to the humbled and stricken capital of the Confederacy. At any rate, he evidently thought that his own return to that city so soon after his departure might be construed as a pleasure trip of idle curiosity. His sensitive nature felt for the defeated South and rebelled against any possible demonstration of vainglory.

Mrs. Lincoln doubtless recognized in the alternative reported to her by her messenger the note of decision that meant finality, for soon afterward the little party continued the journey.

One telegram sent by President Lincoln from City Point to Secretary Stanton contains a sentence which in the light of subsequent events seems pregnant with pathos. I have often read the words and imagined the hopeful, cheerful spirit in which he wrote them.

> HEAD QUARTERS ARMIES OF THE UNITED STATES,
> CITY POINT, April 3, 5 P. M., 1865.
>
> *Hon. Sec. of War, Washington, D. C.*
>
> Yours received. Thanks for your caution; but I have already been to Petersburg, staid with Gen. Grant an hour & a half and returned here. It is certain now that Richmond is in our hands, and I think I will go there to-morrow. I will take care of myself.
>
> A. LINCOLN.

"I will take care of myself." And twelve days later Lincoln was dead.

Gen. Winfield Scott was an old man when the war broke out and wholly incapacitated for active service yet his mature wisdom gained by long experience was an asset of no little moment to the Government in the management and direction of the armies.

When McClellan was placed in command of the Army of the Potomac he flouted the suggestions of his aged superior; for the youthful egotist, swelled mightily by the sense of his vast importance, could brook no man who questioned his omniscience. It might be expected, therefore, that he would scoff at the imbecile Scott and the crude and uncouth Lincoln, who, by some curious defect of comprehension, failed to realize his infallibility. Gen. Scott, naturally sensitive, was hurt by McClellan's disdain. The commander in chief of the Federal forces under direction of the President and Secretary of War, he was deeply wounded by the insolent disregard of his subordinate, who studiously ignored the veteran at Washington. It was perhaps inevitable that one or the other should succumb. And the old warrior gave way. On November 1, 1862, Scott resigned, McClellan succeeding him, to rise and flourish for a while and to fall at length a victim of his own incompetence and conceit.

With General and Mrs. Grant, I attended the commencement exercises at the West Point Military Academy in the spring of 1865. There was a bevy of fair young women present and the occasion was one of rare enjoyment. While Grant was upon the field reviewing the cadets, Mrs. Grant and Gen. Scott, who was then a resident of West Point, sat upon the veranda. I was standing a short distance away an interested spectator of the scene. It must have been that the old soldier inquired my identity, for the good lady called to me and introduced me to her companion in highly flattering words. We shook hands; I remember how very soft was the hand that he extended to me and how gently firm was his clasp. He fixed his piercing black eyes upon mine and said in response to my murmured expression of pleasure:

"I can readily see, Mr. Beckwith, that Gen. Grant's confidence is well reposed."

Scott, at this time, was 79 years old (he died the following year), a feeble and broken relic of a once superb manhood. In his prime he stood close to 6 feet and 6 inches in height and weighed 250 pounds. Now he towered above me by almost a foot, he was still of massive frame; but he was 'in the sere and yellow leaf," wrinkled and worn and tremulous.

I can always recall his face: large and round, with a very broad and full forehead, thick nose and resolute mouth. His eyes, for one so aged, were wonderfully bright and expressive; they seemed the only thing about him that had not gone to decay. His hair was snow white; he wore somewhat exaggerated "sideburns" and a wisp of hair underneath his chin. Verily in the words of the poet: Ere the pruning knife of time cut him down, Not a beter man was found By the crier on his round Through the town.

While we were at West Point Gen. Scott presented to Grant a book, one of his own, and upon the fly leaf he wrote these words, which subsequently I read:

"From the oldest to the greatest General of the Army of the United States."

XII. APRIL THE FOURTEENTH.

The 14th day of April, 1865, stands black in the calendar of American history; for it marks the commission of one of the most heinous crimes ever perpetrated by man, the assassination of Abraham Lincoln.

I was in Washington on the day mentioned with Gen. Grant. Arrangements had been made for the attendance at Ford's Theatre in the evening of a distinguished party. The President and Mrs. Lincoln were to occupy a box at the performance of "Our American Cousin," and they had invited the General and his wife to accompany them. The newspapers chronicled the happy tidings and the announcement was greeted with general approval. The war was done; peace for which the country had waited so many anxious and fearful years was at hand. Joy and thanksgiving were manifest everywhere. The people wanted to see these two intrepid leaders, who, above all others, were responsible for the fruition of their hopes. And doubtless both Lincoln and Grant felt the need of diverting relaxation.

But the life of the great soldier, which had been declared forfeited by the conspirators, was spared to the nation for further usefulness. Secretary Stanton, upon learning of the arrangements for the theatre party, promptly registered most strenuous objections to the plan. He had for some months been aware that threats of assassination were being made by certain evil minded persons against the leaders of the Federal Government and army, and, though not giving full credence to the many reports and rumors, he believed that all reasonable measures should be taken for the safeguarding of the lives of the President, his Cabinet and Generals. Secret service agents in Washington and elsewhere had got wind of several suspicious plots that foreboded ill to our eminent officials. Stanton, accordingly, was wary.

Lincoln knew of some of these threats, but he paid little attention to them. He could not figure out how any one would profit by his death; his successor would carry on the work and the tasks before him would be discharged in any event by others. Then, why assassinate him? He made light of his Secretary's fears and chided him for his lack of faith in human nature. But Stanton was not dissuaded. The presence of the President of the nation and the Lieutenant-General of the armies at any public function at such a critical hour was simply courting disaster.

Gen. Grant was easily persuaded of the indiscretion of such an exposure. As a matter of fact he didn't want to go at all, but had yielded to the President's request to accommodate the Executive. When he learned at the War Department of the fears of Stanton he acquiesced at once in his suggestion that the visit to the playhouse be abandoned; not because of any timidity on his part, but because he wanted to find an excuse for absenting himself from the performance.

On the morning of the 14th, therefore, Grant sent word to the White House that he would withdraw his acceptance of the kind invitation, assigning as his reason that he wished to visit his daughter Nellie, who was attending school in Burlington, N. J. And in the early afternoon the General's party, which included Mrs. Grant and myself, left by rail for the North.[26]

When we reached Philadelphia we left the train and drove to Bloodgood's Hotel. The street was thronged with people and a crowd of men filled the lobby. As we entered and made our way through the throng I felt by the silence that greeted the General and by the stern faces around us that it must be unpleasant news that awaited us. I was about to inquire the cause of the gathering when a man, the night operator I assume he was, stepped forward and handed a telegram to Grant. We walked into the parlor and the three of us, General and Mrs. Grant and I, sat down upon a sofa in one corner of the room. He read the despatch and without comment passed it to his wife, who in turn read it and with an exclamation of painful surprise handed it to me.

I shall never forget the dumb horror of that moment. My heart seemed to leap into my throat. None of us spoke a word. We simply sat there and wondered. Lincoln was shot.

A sudden movement in the crowd attracted my attention. The operator who had delivered the message to Grant raised a finger and beckoned to me and I got up to answer the summons. He took me to one side and pressed into my hand a telegram. It was from Stanton and to me personally. It directed me to have a pilot engine precede our train on its way back to Washington without fail. Was it possible that the Government feared a wholesale attempt upon the lives of our prominent officials? Possibly others besides the President had already fallen beneath an assassin's bullet.

I did not disclose the communication to Grant, for I knew that he would scoff at the order as needless precaution; but I quietly took the necessary steps to carry out the Secretary's injunction.

Before resuming our journey to Burlington I left word at the office to forward to that place immediately any despatches that might come from Washington. I also requested the operator to notify me if he learned of any new developments in the situation.

---

26. For Julia Dent Grant's account of why Grant did not go to the theater, see John Y. Simon, ed., *The Personal Memoirs of Julia Dent Grant* (New York, 1975), 154-56.

Upon reaching the New Jersey town I informed Grant that I was going to sit up the balance of the night.

"In case any message comes, General," I said, "I will be right there on the job to receive it, and I can at once bring it to you if its importance is such as to warrant it."

He didn't like the idea. "You had better go to bed," he suggested, "and get some sleep. Let the messages go till morning."

For the first and only time while I was in his service I disobeyed him. I stayed in the telegraph office until 6 o'clock A. M. of the 15th, not knowing what strange events might be happening at the capital; but it was a fruitless vigil; nothing of any interest came over the wire.

After breakfast Gen. Grant, his brother-in-law, Gen. F. T. Dent, and I took a train for Washington. Little was said by any of us during the long hours that followed.

Gen. Halleck met us at the station upon our arrival in Washington (we had now learned of the President's death and of the vicious assault on Seward) and we drove in a closed carriage to the War Department. Grant went at once to Stanton's private office, while Halleck and I remained outside in the corridor. For several minutes the General paced nervously up and down before me, apparently laboring under much worriment. At length he paused and, turning to me, said:

"Beckwith, I wish you would warn Gen. Grant against going to Willard's Hotel. That is where he usually stops and it is generally known. He ought to avoid publicity at this time and keep out of danger. There is no telling what might happen to him."

I told him that I thought it would be presumptuous in me to advise the Lieutenant-General as to any course of conduct but that if he desired me to convey a message to Grant. I would gladly do so.

"Then do so," he replied; "give him my warning as a message from me."

When Gen. Grant came from the Secretary's office, I met him and we walked together from the building and toward the White House. I imparted Halleck's forebodings to him in front of the Executive Mansion. He had been walking in thoughtful silence with his eyes upon the ground. Now he looked up at me and said:

"I guess, Beckwith, if they want me, they'll get me wherever I am. We'll go to Willard's."

And go we did. So much for Halleck's fears.

Ever mindful of the anxiety of his family for his welfare, Grant, upon our arrival in the city, had directed me to send a telegram to his wife at Burlington, notifying her of his safety. This I did in the following message:

WAR DEPARTMENT,
WASHINGTON, D. C., April 15, '65.

Mrs. U. S. Grant, Burlington, N. J.:

I am requested by the Lieutenant-General to inform you of his safe arrival. Please inform Mrs. Dent. The President died this morning. There are still hopes of Secretary Seward's recovery.

S. H. BECKWITH.

I have oftentimes since marvelled at the stoicism of this remarkable man, in whose hands peculiarly had been and was the salvation of the Union. The fearful blow that had been given the nation in the murder of the President and the attack upon Seward must have been a terrible shock to him, yet throughout all those trying hours, when the passions of men were at fever heat, when suspicion was rife that he himself had been marked for assassination, Grant maintained unbroken his inscrutable reserve. Doubtless he felt as keenly as any of us, probably more than most of us, the irreparable loss the country had sustained, but his innate reticence, his iron will, prevented any outward display.

Abraham Lincoln! Quaint, simple, humble, masterful, truly great; raised up by an omniscient God to lead us through the wilderness of strife, and when we were safely through, taken by Him to receive the reward that is given to them who serve faithfully both God and men. This world will never see a kindlier, nobler, braver, wiser man.

XIII. The Pursuit of the Assassin.

I remained in Washington until the 22d of April, when I was ordered to the lower Potomac to establish communication by telegraph with the War Department and keep the authorities in touch with the several parties that had been detailed to that section to search for Booth, the assassin. It was rumored that he had passed through Maryland in his flight and was somewhere in hiding near Point Lookout, at the mouth of the Potomac River. I left the capital on the river boat Keystone, taking with me as my only companion a lineman whom I expected to use in tapping and repairing the wire in case of emergency. Pursuant to orders, I made my way to Port Tobacco, a little hamlet on Tobacco Creek in southern Maryland, arriving there at 1 o'clock the next morning, Monday, April 24.

The first thing that I did was to secure lodgings and turn in for a few hours' sleep. After an early breakfast I set out a-horse to find Major James R. O'Beirne, who, with a small command, had been hurried southward soon after the shooting, and who had been prosecuting diligent search for the fugitive. I had proceeded but a short distance when I met the Major returning from a quest which he had conducted with substantial results. We dismounted and he gave me the latest news of the probable whereabouts of Booth and his accessory, Herold. I at once galloped back to the telegraph line, tapped the wire and sent this despatch to Washington:

PORT TOBACCO, Md.,
April 24, 1865—10 A. M.

Major Eckert:

Have just met Major O'Beirne, whose force had arrested Dr. Mudd and Thompson. Mudd set Booth's left leg (fractured), furnished crutches and helped him and Herold off. They have been tracked as far as the swamp near Bryantown, and, under one theory, it is possible that they may be still concealed in swamp, which leads from Bryantown to Allen's Fresh; or in neck of land between Wicomico and Potomac rivers. Other evidence leads to the belief that they crossed from Swan's Point to White Point, Va., on Sunday morning, April 16, about 9:30 in a small boat, also captured by Major O'Beirne. John M. Lloyd has been arrested and virtually acknowledged complicity. I will continue with Major O'Beirne, in whom I have very great confidence. We propose first to thoroughly scour swamp and country to-day, and if unsuccessful and additional evidence will justify it we then propose to cross with force into Virginia and follow up that trail as long as there is any hope. At all events we will keep moving, and if there is any chance you may rely upon our making most of it. Country here is being thoroughly scoured by infantry and cavalry.

I feel a pardonable pride in the authorship of this message, although, of course, Major O'Beirne supplied me with the material. It is really of considerable historical importance, because from it the clue was derived which resulted in the capture of the murderer.

Secretary Stanton, promptly upon its receipt, ordered Lieut. E. P. Doherty, of the 16th New York Cavalry, to proceed with all possible speed to Port Tobacco. As fortune decreed, it was Doherty and his men who had the honor of ridding the land of the cowardly fanatic and capturing his companion. But O'Beirne and I did not idly await their coming.

After sending the above telegram, the Major and I with his command rode to Bryantown to take up the track of Booth, if possible, and run him to earth. It wasn't the easiest task in the world to trace the flight of the conspirators.

When we reached the village, we learned after considerable inquiry that Booth and Herold had, within a few hours, called at the home of a Mr. Turner, a country gentleman residing a couple of miles to the north, and asked for food; so we rode out to the house indicated to verify the report. We found that it was true. Two of the servants told us that a hungry looking fellow with an injured leg and crutches and another who answered Herold's description had called at the door that day and begged for something to eat. Upon leaving, they had entered the pine thicket back of the house and disappeared from view.

Here was something tangible to work on. The Major deployed his men and we immediately penetrated the thicket, like a pack of hounds trying to pick up the trail. I was the first to find the telltale clue, the impress of a stick in a portion of soft earth. It was made by the crutch of the wounded Booth, who was hobbling along as best he could, striving to escape the fate that followed him like Nemesis. The track led in a circuitous direction toward a piece of timber, where we lost it and in spite of painstaking endeavor were unable to [f]ind it again. If we could only have utilized the services of a trained bloodhound at that time our efforts would have been, I am sure, crowned with success; but we had to depend upon our own astuteness and hence failed.

There was no doubt in the Major's mind, nor in mine either, that Booth was somewhere near by concealed in the underbrush; but his hiding place was too well covered for our discovery.

At half past 1 o'clock on the morning of April 26 I sent a telegram to Major Eckert summarizing our day's labors and suggesting a better system in the arrangement and employment of the troops who had been assigned to the man hunt. My suggestion, however, was made too late for adoption; the pursuit was ended.

As soon as Lieut. Doherty arrived upon the scene of action I gave him all the information I had, and he and his party had on the same night (the 25th) gone in the direction of Bowling Green, Va. While we were engaged as above described, the lieutenant's detail caught the trail afresh and traced it to the lair. The rest of the story is familiar history.

Thus, while I personally was not with the command that avenged the death of our beloved President, I feel that I can claim the honor of assisting in furnishing the clue that led to the avengement. And the fact that I received $500 of the reward offered for the apprehension of Booth is pretty good proof of my claim.

Conclusion.

With the garrulity of an old soldier, I presume that I could go on with my narration of events and descriptions of men until I had exhausted the patience of the reader. But I realize that there is a limit to all things as there is to life, which cannot now be far away for me. In the preparation of these memoirs, I have lived again those wonderful years that timed the death struggle of secession and slavery. Before me have passed the mighty armies that are no more. I have seen again their generals and heard them speak. I have been with my old commander, the unconquerable Grant, on his campaigns. I have stood beside the noble Lincoln and looked upon his wan and anxious face. They are gone now and I am done. Permit me to conclude by appending an appreciation of my poor efforts and unwavering faithfulness. When I left the service, Gen. Grant wrote me the following letter. Needless to say, I prize it among my dearest possessions:

HEADQUARTERS ARMIES OF THE UNITED STATES.
WASHINGTON, D. C., Feb. 19th, 1866.

S. H. Beckwith,

DEAR SIR—Now that you are about leaving the service of the Unted States after more than four years continuous duty, it affords me pleasure to bear testimony to the efficient manner in which you performed your duties.

Enlisting early in the war, as a private soldier, you were, in 1862, if my memory serves me right, detailed in special duty at my headquarters as telegraph operator. Performing your duties faithfully you were discharged in 1863 as a soldier to take employment with the army as operator, and was soon after placed in over all other operators at Headquarters. Soon after the army cipher was intrusted to you. From that time to the close of the rebellion, no reason ever existed for relieving you from the confidential position of cipher operator, thus intrusting to your knowledge every despatch, order and information of such importance as to demand being communicated so that none should know of them but those for whom they were intended, and hence you were continued in your position.

Now that you leave the public service for private pursuits, I wish you every success, and in the position of telegraph employee, any capacity, do not hesitate to recommend you.

Yours truly,
U. S. GRANT, Lieut.-General.

Index